3

GAMES
PRISONERS
PLAY

GAMES
PRISONERS
PLAY
The Tragicomic
Worlds of
Polish Prison

Marek M.
KAMINSKI

PRINCETON UNIVERSITY PRESS

PRINCETON AND OXFORD

ISBN: 0-691-11721-7

British Library Cataloging-in-Publication Data is available
This book has been composed in Galliard with Helvetica
Designed by Lorraine Doneker and composed by Gary R. Beck
Printed on acid-free paper. ∞

www.pupress.princeton.edu

Printed in the United States of America

10 9 8 7 6 5 4 3 2 1

TO MY PARENTS AND SISTER

Contents

Figures

Tables

Acknowledgments

Many people contributed in many ways to this research and book. I acknowledge their contributions in a more or less chronological manner.

During seven years that I spent as an underground Solidarity publisher, I worked most closely with Joanna Dąbrowska, Agnieszka Gutkowska, John Hall, Jr., Krzysztof Kawiecki, Ewa and Robert Kępczyńscy, Jarek Komorowski, Darek Okoń, Beata Oliwa, Wojtek Pawlak, Adam and Tomek Peszke, Leszek Robakiewicz, Andrzej Sadowski, Sławek Salamon, Kasia and Tadzinek Winkowscy, Jacek and Bożena Wycech, and Aleksandra Wysocka. I am grateful to all of them, and to hundreds of other people for the privilege of working with them for a free and democratic Poland.

My parents Elżbieta and Mikołaj Kamińscy and my sister Basia themselves smuggled many documents out of prison and set up a smuggling channel with the help of an anonymous guard. I received other invaluable assistance from Henryk Banaszak, Amnesty International, the Catholic Church Primate's Committee and Bishop Dąbrowski, my lawyer Andrzej Grabiński, Jadwiga Staniszkis, Zosia Rybińska, Władysława Szubert, and Tomek Właszczuk. Doctor Possart, the head of the Rakowiecka prison surgical department, suggested the successful plan of faking a major sickness. He was later supported by Dr. Wróbel and Professor Kułakowski.

My sociology advisor in graduate school, Antoni Kamiński, first suggested applying game theory. My online conversations with Diego Gambetta revived my interest in prison behavior. Then, I was lucky to meet the perfect editor—Ian Malcolm of Princeton University Press—who helped me enormously with polishing the book's English and accepted my various nonstandard requests. Mirek Andrzejewski, who himself spent many months behind bars in Poland as a political prisoner in the 1980s, provided wonderful illustrations. The final manuscript benefitted from the comments of Steven Brams, Youssef Cohen, Dominika Dzięgielewska, Matt Golder, Grzegorz Lissowski, Joe Oppenheimer, Piotr Swistak, Katherine Tate, the anonymous referees and, especially, Monika Nalepa, with whom I discussed all details and ideas at each stage of writing.

My research was supported by fellowships and grants from ICPSR at the University of Michigan, Ann Arbor, the Institute for Humane Studies, and the Center for the Study of Democracy at the University of California, Irvine. Two former chairmen of the Politics department at New York University, Russell Hardin and George Downs, provided me with much needed financial help when the Immigration and Naturalization relegated me for a two-year exile from NYU.

Finally, this research would have been impossible without the collective hard work of thousands of anonymous policemen, prosecutors, and judges who tirelessly jailed and imprisoned thousands of Polish and other Eastern European dissidents during the reign of communism. Their efforts are unlikely ever to get the attention they deserve.

Introduction

Prison socializes an inmate to behave hyperrationally. It teaches him patience in planning and pursuing his goals, punishes him severely for his mistakes, and rewards him generously for smart action. No wonder that inmates are such ardent optimizers. A clever move can shorten one's sentence, save one from rape or a beating, keep one's spirit high, or increase one's access to resources. There is little space for innocent and spontaneous expressions of emotion when they collide with fundamental interests. Brutal fights, self-injury, and rapes can all be explained as outcomes of carefully calculated actions. Paradoxically, much of the confusion in interpreting prison behavior arises from both a failure to understand the motives of inmates and an unwillingness to admit that outcomes judged as inhuman or bizarre may be consequences of individually rational action.

The main message of the book is that prisoners optimize under the constraints of their harsh life conditions and the local subculture. Their behavior reflects their attempts at optimization. Such a "rational choice" approach helps us to better understand prison behavior.

A Personal Note—How Did I Obtain Access to My Data?

I beg the reader's forgiveness for a brief personal narrative that explains how I learned this lesson myself, and how I collected the data that support it. This is not an autobiography, but I would not be writing this book had I not experienced the life of a prisoner firsthand.

In 1985 I was a twenty-two-year-old sophomore student of sociology who had switched disciplines, disappointed with abstract concepts after three diligent years of studying math. Poland had just witnessed the glorious rise of the Solidarity movement in 1980 followed by the introduction of martial law under General Jaruzelski in 1981 with the rationale that can be summarized as "I kicked your ass, but the Soviets would shoot it." Dissatisfied with the moral and esthetic poverty of communist way of life, I joined the underground Solidarity resistance network. In 1985, I was running an underground publishing house, *STOP* that employed about twenty full-time workers and up to 100 moonlighters. Between 1982 and 1989, we published about thirty-five titles of more than 100,000 books combined. We were a part of a decentralized network that included about 100 underground publishing houses, hundreds of periodicals, thousands of trade union organizations with a hierarchically organized leadership structure, a few Nobel prize winners, and even underground theaters, galleries, and video rentals. We called it an "independent society."

Half-revolutionist, half-scholar in the making, I was also looking for a topic for my Masters thesis in social anthropology. With hesitation, I started collecting data on the inner workings of the resistance network. My dilemma was figuring out how to balance facts with fiction. If too accurate, my thesis could easily become a handbook for the communist secret police. After my thesis defense I could also fall under permanent surveillance, effectively preventing me from running my organization. At the very worst, the communist court could use my thesis as evidence and throw me in prison.

On March 12, 1985 my thesis dilemma was solved. During a random stop at a police checkpoint, "Dragon," the driver of our van, was so nervous that the policeman became suspicious. He disregarded Dragon's fake documents and implemented a thorough search of the van, which was filled with illegal Solidarity books. Dragon decided to talk. Within hours, five secret police agents had escorted me to a police station, joking that "you will have to swim, Mr. Marek." In fact, I was "swimming"—police jargon for jail sentence—for five months in the Bialoleka and Rakowiecka jails. On my second day in a police station cell, after overcoming my initial shock and disbelief, I decided that my thesis would be on the subculture of Polish prison.

After just several hours I knew that I was entering a bizarre, terrifying, and incredibly interesting environment. Rapes, knife fights, suicides, brutal sex, blunt talk, and self-injuries appeared to be its chief attributes. Ordinary life was reduced to eating and defecating. It seemed as if Pandora had freed all the imaginable violent human emotions from her box there and let them play without the usual societal constraints.

I decided to make the best of my personal misfortune and use it as a unique opportunity to study this fascinating society-within-society. My goals were clear: I did not want to write nostalgic memoirs or point an accusing finger at the regime that had jailed me. I wanted to conduct an extensive and uncompromising research project, using all of my methodological skills. I expected that this would require developing new research techniques or modifying old ones. I was ready to face the necessary risks. It was up to me whether I mobilized my academic spirit—or gave up and slipped into the monotony of day-to-day prison life. I estimated that I would be in prison for up to three years, enough time for a comprehensive field study. Surprisingly, "researching prison" turned out to be an excellent survival strategy. Mentally, it kept me in good shape in the face of adversity—since adversity facilitated fast learning. My research spared me from the helpless repetitions of the "What-am-I-doing-here?" question that introspective characters like to invoke on life's meanders. It helped me to socialize into my new role as an inmate and, at the same time, maintain a healthy distance from it. If you, my reader, are ever unfortunate enough to be jailed, I highly recommend the strategy of "researching prison."

Following my release, I wrote a couple of term papers, some drafts of which had earlier been smuggled out of jail, my thesis, and a few research articles. However, during all that time I suffered from intellectual discomfort and felt that my grasp of prison life remained inadequate. The available prison literature and inmate memoirs offered fascinating details and stories but were of little help in understanding the general mechanisms. It took me nearly three years to find what I thought was a promising methodological approach—game theory. Trying to model prison interactions as games, I completed my formerly abandoned mathematical studies with a specialization in game theory. I became a game theorist and, from time to time, tried to construct prison games.

I wrote this book to correct what I perceived to be the failure of my earlier research. In effect, this book summarizes my recurring attempts to interpret and understand my prison experience over seventeen years. I believe that the galaxy of random anecdotes that I have collected can be condensed into a coherent system. Game theory seems to be well-suited for capturing the spirit of inmate interactions. Games, decision problems, or just informal descriptions of strategic interactions convey the message that I was struggling to formulate at the time of my thesis. With all its weirdness and inhuman appearance, prison behavior is the product of rational persons who calculate the consequences of their actions and try to maximize their payoffs subject to environmental constraints. The goal of my book is to enhance this message, in addition to providing an ethnographic description of prison codes, argot, and customs.[1]

WHAT THIS BOOK ATTEMPTS TO DO

The book reconstructs various components of the subculture of *grypsmen*, the highest inmate caste in Polish prisons, and provides a set of formal and informal models representing strategic interactions that arise in the presence of subcultural and other constraints. The main components of subculture include initiation rituals, various explicitly formulated norms regulating the behavior of grypsmen, secret argot vocabulary and grammar, techniques of exchanging information and goods, prison art and entertainment, and techniques of faking and self-injuring. Within the strategic environment defined by prison constraints and subculture, I focus on specific games, decision situations, and tests that characterize prison life.

Formal models help us to convert the enormous complexity of social interactions into more manageable forms. While the price for modeling is always paid in simplification, a good model may offer surprising benefits. For instance, many cases of prison rape follow an inmate's failure to pass a tricky initiation test that is routinely applied to some rookies. There are immediate policy consequences of such a proposition. Revealing the existence of such a test to new inmates could automatically reduce the number of rapes. As the reader will later learn, an informed inmate passes virtually all tests effortlessly.

Although the number of strategic situations described here is large, I develop only a handful of formal models. There is a good reason for doing this: simplicity. Quite often I abandoned formalism entirely when its use might obscure my main point. A model is useful when it clarifies the structure of interactions and when it has sufficiently wide applicability. In cases of initiation tests, relatively simple models satisfy both criteria. In cases such as the "dirty physiology norms" separating eating from defecating or farting, formalization would rarely enhance the reader's insight. Moreover, it would make the description dramatically boring. An informally stated argument: "Scarcity of space, slow airflow, low food quality introduce strong incentives for coordination on defecation and farting norms" seems to capture the point sufficiently well. Some of the stories that I tell have so many idiosyncratic features that a relevant formal model would represent this particular story only. Building a model to explain such stories would be like hunting for a fly with a revolver. Nevertheless, the story may be interesting and important enough to tell it without formalization. Again, my main goal is not to overformalize what can be said simply.

WHAT THIS BOOK DOES NOT ATTEMPT TO DO

The "closed" prison environment makes collecting quantitative data extremely difficult, if at all possible. Inmates implement so many methods of lying and misrepresentation that surveys or other techniques are often rendered almost useless. Without hard data, rigorous testing of any empirical hypotheses with appropriate statistical tools is not possible. While this book offers various empirical hypotheses, in addition to case studies and models of interactions, it does not attempt to rigorously test any such hypotheses.

Some of the prison constraints are defined by the physical conditions of the prison environment and the penal system. Others are subcultural and their evolution into the final form is particularly hard to explain. I do not aim to explain the changes of systems of norms and rules and their relation with prison constraints. The rational choice approach does not work very well when dealing with the evolution of complex norms, with multiple iterations, incomplete information, or inadequate beliefs. It works best when there are simple constraints, repeatable and standardized interactions, and full—at least on one side—information.

The reader may also be disappointed in the scarcity of comparison with other prison systems. I included a small number of comparative references but decided not to develop systematic comparisons, as this is the subject for a different work.

HOW I COLLECTED MY DATA: OBSERVING PARTICIPANT VERSUS PARTICIPANT OBSERVATION

The prison subculture is immensely difficult to penetrate. Inmates carefully protect information, because they know that the frivolous disclosure of a secret may prolong an inmate's prison sentence, jeopardize his parole, lower his status among comrades, cut off access to resources, or reveal that sickness is simulated. Inmates develop ingenious methods of cheating on one another, on guards, physicians, or psychologists. Techniques of *deciphering* other inmates are applied in order to identify squealers. A sociologist using a questionnaire in Polish prisons is usually confused with a prison psychologist. Survey answers commonly reflect an inmate's perception of his own self-interest against a person who is perceived as a part of the prison administration. A typical inmate spends a lot of time with his cellmates working out answers to anticipated psychologists' questions that would work best for his case. Such an environment "defends itself against research."[2]

The main broadly defined source of data was, naturally, my own experience as an *observing participant* (OP). I define this particular research role, in contrast to *participant observation*, with two conditions: (a) OP enters a community through a similar social process as its other members and is subject to similar rules; (b) OP undertakes field research *as if* he or she was a researcher. An ideal OP lives through his/her social role, impassively registers randomly generated personal experience, and applies available data gathering techniques.[3]

Epistemology of Participation versus Observation

A participant or a participating observer may gather useful data when more formalized methods of data collection are not available or provide unreliable output. A participant perceives his world differently than a participating observer perceives the domain of his study. Differences in beliefs, access to information, and attitudes of these two related roles lead to role-specific epistemological deformations. Such typical deformations are briefly characterized below.

A participant is personally interested in his story. He avoids topics that are inconvenient for him and "forgets" embarrassing facts. A political prisoner emphasizes his own heroism against an unjust regime. A criminal prisoner claims innocence against an unjust court. Both of them believe, after Solzhenitsyn, Bukovsky, and others, that "only a prisoner will understand another prisoner."[4] In other words, a typical inmate hardly considers his prison experience to be intersubjectively communicable. He rarely applies any standardized techniques of data gathering. Instead, he focuses on anecdotes and interprets events through his own experience.

A participant observer lacks the sense of real-life pressure participants experience. He is not as affected emotionally by the events as a participant. He lacks experiences that can stimulate one's understanding of insiders' problems. In prison, such experience includes the stress of being arrested, interrogated, or transferred to another prison. He may be unaware that inmates use incredibly ingenious techniques to decipher squealers and that such techniques are applied routinely to newbies. Inmates may check his background, his papers and timing of various events, his contacts in his previous prisons and in the "freedom world," and where he lived and worked.[5] They monitor his in-cell and out-of-cell activities. Most likely, he will be deciphered in a matter of minutes in a new cell. There is an interesting correlation here: one can learn most from those inmates who are most likely to decipher him. Despite all of my precautions, I was "deciphered" twice by my cellmates as a "sociologist who takes notes and does research in prison." In one case, a beating followed. All that occurred despite the fact that I was a true inmate, that my research was only a by-product of my role, and that I knew both the argot and prison norms well.

Sources of Data

My data sources can be sorted into a few categories: (i) Living through various inmate roles; (ii) Informal evening tea chats; (iii) Secret code training of grypsmen candidates; (iv) Informal conversations with inmates, typically face-to-face; (v) Prison artifacts such as pictures, songs, letters, and hand-made products; (vi) The memoirs and written relations of political and criminal prisoners and conversations with former political prisoners; (vii) Underground Solidarity research reports on prisons and uncensored Warsaw University working papers and officially released statistical data.

The data were collected over five months of imprisonment in thirteen cells of two jails, including three police station and court cells. I met about 190 inmates and developed some form of close relationship with about 140 inmates (see table I.1). In references to the sources of my data that appear in the text, I provide the cell number where the relevant data were collected.

I recorded data using various means. Note-taking in prison is extremely difficult. Prisoners prohibit and punish cellmates for writing down any account of cell activity. Guards try to seize the notes on the inmate's way out and during routine searches of the cell. Writing standardized regular daily reports was impossible. Initially, I secretly recorded my observations and argot vocabulary on

TABLE I.1.
My Cells

Nr	Date	Destination	Mn	Mt	Ar	Nh
1	3/12	Wilcza police station	6	5	15	1
2	3/13	Cyryl and Metody police station	6	6	12	2
3	3/15	Court sorting cell	7	6	20	—
		Bialoleka Jail				31
4	3/15	Temporary sorting cell	4	3	14.5	3
5	3/18	Health emergency cell	1	0	10	7
6	3/25	Regular cell	9	8	14.5	21
		Rakowiecka Jail				115
7	4/15	Internal medicine cell	6	9	20	24
8	5/9	Regular cell	8	8	9	7
9	5/16	Surgery cell 1	6	8	20	18
10	6/3	Surgery cell 2	6	7	20	14
11	6/17	Surgery emergency cell	3	3	12	7
12	6/24	Surgery cell 3	7	6	20	32
13	7/26	Regular large cell (*barn*)	45	50	50	14
	8/9	Release				
		Total		119		149

Note: Nr = consecutive cell number; some dates are approximate (±1–2 days), year = 1985; Mn = estimated average number of inmates per cell (including the author); Mt = estimated total number of inmates met in the cell; Ar = estimated cell area, in m²; Nh = number of nights spent in the cell. Total number of inmates met in cells: about 119. Corridormen and inmates met in transport, walkspaces, or other places outside cells: about 70.

scraps of paper, often while all of the other inmates went for a walk, trying to hide the notes before their curious eyes. A few notes were destroyed, but later reconstructed. Once I received a beating; however, in most cells after a few days my writing was tolerated and confused with "studying." I took some notes in English, a truly foreign language for most inmates. The "English lessons" that I offered voluntarily to inmates also served as a cover-up. No paper document was ever seized by prison personnel.

Copies of the notes were prepared before expected family visits, my principal smuggling channel. Next, these media were placed in a specially prepared shoe or in underwear, taken to the visiting room, and smuggled out of prison for safe storage. As a backup, I mailed numerous letters to my family with descriptions of those aspects of prison life that could make it through the prison censorship. The first set of notes was expedited as a secret message with the help of a fellow inmate as an apology for an unjustified beating. A few notes were smuggled by a helpful guard who was recruited by my sister.

Another useful technique was borrowed from Solzhenitsyn.[6] Every evening, before falling asleep, I repeated all of the new words, rules, customs, jokes, little games, or self-injury techniques that I had learned during that day. An extra benefit of this routine was a fast socialization to the inmate life.

My prison experience was so intense that after my release it allowed me to reconstruct many of the crucial interactions and facts with great precision. For more than one year after release, all of my night dreams revolved around prison facts, events, and people. Over the period of 2.5 years, I wrote down all memories that were not recorded previously and assembled them into a small archive including an argot dictionary and catalogs of initiation tests and techniques of self-injury. I completed five term papers, about ten short prison stories, three interviews and roundtables for the underground Solidarity press, and a Master of Arts thesis in sociology.

The four principal sources of data are discussed below in more detail.

Research-Through-a-Role

I went through the social roles of rookie (twice), humiliated rookie, potential sucker, aproposman, grypsman,[7] self-injury expert, faker, and tough political prisoner. Among the major inmate roles that I did not experience were fag, squealer, corridorman, elder, fuss-master, cat, and jumper.

In addition to all of the routine cell activities, the catalog of social situations I experienced includes interrogation, family meetings, transport, conversations with all ranks of prison personnel, conflict over the status of a political prisoner with guards and warden, punitive reports, help from a guard and physicians, the company of recidivists and juveniles, tea infusion drug effects, losing all belongings in poker, thievery of my tea and other goods, bridge and chess marathons, a beating, an involuntary haircut, a squealer's intrigue, a fag's threat, masturbation, extensive cell trade, intercell communication, smuggling goods and secret documents out and in as well as all major illegal activities, escape planning, armed escort to a freedom hospital, training to become a professional thief, light self-injury, and the successful management of my own faking game. I was subject to fag-making, baptism, and almost all of the other tests described in the book.

Major situations that I did not experience include hardbed solitary confinement, tattooing, beating during interrogation, contact with a lawyer, homosexual intercourse, group masturbation, a love affair, a sucker or fag's attack, and a hunger protest.

An activist attitude helps enormously with collecting data. I tried to assist with all of the meaningful cell activities, such as tattooing, the production of prison artifacts, playing chess and bridge. When possible, I tried to initiate such activities. A risky idea was the experimental breaking of various subcultural and administrative rules. Such experiments included refusing to enter the walkplace from the prison backyard, shouting anticommunist slogans, drawing anticommunist symbols in the walkplaces, and so on. The punishment was so severe that I quickly abandoned this learning channel.

Evening Tea Chats and Informal Conversations

Sykes regards "the relatively "unstructured" talks with the captors and their captives [as] the most useful [source of data] by far, despite the dangers introduced by a lack of standardization and undoubted biases of selection."[8] I concur and consider informal talks and chats as a data source on par with the "research-through-the-role" and secret training.

A great source for learning prison customs and argot were about fifty evening *tea chats* on prison subculture that I used to initiate and that usually engaged the entire cell. As an incentive for inmates to join a tea chat I provided free *czajura*, which is a tea infusion that was illegal in Polish jails in 1985. Czajura works as a soft drug, stimulates memory, and sparks long conversations. It worked as an invaluable research device, creating incentives for in-depth conversations on prison matters. I traded most of my prison account money, personal belongings and, especially, Amnesty International's humanitarian packages for tea packets.

Face-to-face conversations were especially helpful in uncovering inmate self-injury and faking goals and plans. My credentials as a political prisoner, basic medical knowledge learned from my parents, who are physicians, and, last but not least, a willingness to listen made me a desirable confidant. In almost all cases, inmates revealed their secrets only after one-week- or two-week-long interactions.

A simple principle of "path-independence" that I applied in all chats was to free my mind from any assumptions that could make my learning process dependent on previously heard stories or interpretations. It helped to compare versions of customs reported by various sources without overweighting the first source. I tried to limit my chatting contribution to questions, motivating signs of appreciation, and declarations of surprise.

Secret Code Training

The best source of most secret norms and argot rules is a grypsmen night training, described in detail in chapter 3. Its goal is to transmit efficiently all of the secret knowledge to grypsmen candidates. In striking contrast to inmate interviews, instructors have incentives to convey concisely the letter and spirit of the code rather than feed the listener with fairy tales. They even punish slow learners! Learning through lectures by prison sages, eager to share all their wisdom with a curious student, is the researcher's dream. The only problem is that night training sessions steal one's sleeping time. After a few half-night long iterations a researcher may be ready to trade all of his data for a few hours of good sleep.

I participated in about 10–15 hours of secret training in cell 6, about 5 hours in cell 8, and about 30–40 hours in cell 13 (see table I.1).

BOOK ORGANIZATION

This book can be read by someone who is not interested in game theory or by a game theorist willing to enhance his or her lecture with examples outside of economics or political science. Of course,

I wholeheartedly encourage every reader to give game theory a chance. Appendix 1, which briefly discusses some ideas behind games and decisions, may be helpful to set the basic concepts. However, the appendix is obviously not a substitute for a good basic course in game theory. No recommendation is too strong for undertaking this intellectual experience if one is interested in studying social phenomena. Appendix 1 also outlines a formal justification for some of the nonstandard models used in the book. Most importantly, such models include games with no common knowledge, where two players have a different understanding of the game's rules.

All substantive chapters except for the overview in chapter 2, The Constraints of Prison Life, are motivated by a specific class of situations that are associated with various informational characteristics. In Entry (chaper 1) an inmate faces a deceptively simple decision problem that provides a good introduction to his future dilemmas. In his first contact with dwellers of a new cell, he must declare his caste membership. The crux of the situation in chapter 3, Becoming a Grypsman, is the informational asymmetry between old inmates and a rookie. This asymmetry is exploited by the former to test the rookie. In chapters 4 and 5, Prison Code of Behavior and Argot, respectively, various norms and language conventions with varying degrees of secrecy are described. An inmate who passes the initiation tests learns these norms and conventions in a systematic way during night sessions of "prison university." In Everyday Life (chapter 6) an inmate uses skills that are more esoteric and more difficult to teach. He plays against his peers subject to subcultural constraints and tries to entertain himself. When he looks for Sex, Flirtation, Love (chapter 7), his preferences may fluctuate over time chaotically and he may pre-commit himself to temporal celibacy. He displays great ingenuity to satisfy his erotic needs. Chapter 8, Strategic Ailment, is an inmate's action of last resort. He usually makes relevant decisions alone and chooses suffering when no other way of advancing his important goals seems feasible. In Exit (chapter 9) he must quickly deal with the surprise of unexpected release and try to avoid the last hot farewell. The Postscriptum comments on the variants and evolution of the grypsmen subculture.

Numerous conventions appear in the text. Often, I refer to myself as "Student," which was my prison nickname. This convention emphasizes my intention to use my own personal experience as a valuable source of unique data rather than a starting point for reflection or existential speculation. Original material is usually presented with references to "cell *n*," where *n* may be an integer between 1 and 13 and refers to one of the cells listed in table 1.1. Universal or secret *argot* names introduced for the first time, or reintroduced after several pages, are italicized. When the reader needs to look up a particular word quickly, the Glossary of Essential Argot offers key definitions. Argot terms that are self-explanatory are italicized but do not appear in the glossary. Almost all inmates in this book are males. Females, who are usually incarcerated in separate facilities, comprise only a tiny proportion of the prison population in Poland. Their codes of behavior appear to be less complex than those of men.

• • •

A note to the reader: Once I was transferred to an Emergency Room hospital cell. One of my new cellmates was recovering from an operation that removed four pounds of iron from his stomach. He died later after swallowing bedsprings again. Another cellmate was cut off a suicide rope just before he could die. The third, seriously sick with acute pancreatitis, was "doomed to go," according to a "well-informed" guard. All those poor creatures tried to impress the doctors with their symptoms, strategically cried from pain in the night, or pretended the lack of appetite while secretly borrowing food from me.

On Sunday, the day that Polish radio broadcast Catholic mass, I asked the guard to lend us his radio. Listening to mass in prison comforts even the worst sinners and most nonreligious souls. Usually, one may listen to it on Sunday morning in regular cells, but no speaker was installed in our ER. The good-hearted guard, hesitant, took a long look at the four barely alive skeletons, sighed, and said "ok." He disconnected his large box and brought it to our cell for two hours. I installed it and asked my buddies: Do you really want to listen to the mass? "Whatever," they said. They did not care. Then I quickly tuned it to find "Radio Free Europe," the anti-communist radio station funded by Americans. My cellmates, all in plaster and bandages, were delighted. They laughed so hard that I became anxious about their sick stomachs and post-surgery stitches. For two hours, we were laughing and listening to the news from the free world.

Throughout this book, people suffer, die, fight, cheat each other, engage in brutal sex, and make hell out of other mortals' lives. And they laugh. My inclusion of their humor does not make the book less serious. The laughter does not nullify inmates' suffering. The laughter does not redeem their guilt. It only makes their lives more bearable.

CHAPTER ONE

Entry

"ARE YOU A GRYPSMAN?" Every newcomer entering a cell in a Polish jail or prison must answer this fundamental question. He may be moving to a new cell within the same prison or coming from a remote facility. He may be also a *rookie*, still in shock after "they" had caught him.[1] Just after the guard shoves him into the cell and closes the *gate*, he faces an apparently trivial decision problem: He must announce his caste membership to the other inmates in the cell. Yet the strategic considerations involved in answering this simple question are amazingly complex.

A typical rookie has almost certainly heard something about *grypsing* and *grypsmen*, possibly from a helpful soul at a police station, in the main court's *segregator* cell, or in transfer. Grypsmen constitute the majority of inmates and dominate the lower castes, *suckers* and *fags*. Grypsmen are the "tough and smart" boys. They stick together for good and bad. Few inmates entering a prison cell would not like to join this cast. A rookie typically assumes that the inquiring inmate is a grypsman and represents a cell's majority. He is usually correct since a prevailing number of jail cells are *grypsing*. He may be inclined to say "Yes, friends, I am a grypsman, I am one of you" and let this innocent lie help him to do his time in peace.

If he says "yes," he makes a mistake. A grypsman may simply answer "yes" under less important circumstances but not at such a critical moment as entering a new cell. In a typical cell with a majority of grypsmen, such an answer immediately triggers an investigation. The rookie's lie is discovered in a flash. If he is lucky, he gets a couple of forehead blows and is instructed to tell the truth. Another lie and he might lose eligibility for grypsing and become a sucker or, even worse, a fag. If his answers are not satisfactory, he may become one anyway.

So what about a "no" answer? This will not save him from further questioning. If he is a sucker or a fag, he will immediately be shown the physical space he is entitled to and objects that he cannot touch. His place in the cell's hierarchy will be clearly defined. If he is just a rookie, he will be asked a follow-up question whether he wants to become a grypsman. Now, an affirmative answer will initiate the process of checking his eligibility for grypsing. He will be instructed that nobody can answer "no" to the fundamental "are-you-a-grypsman?" question. Those who are not grypsmen are suckers or fags. An answer "I am willing to become a grypsman" does a better job. But even such an answer will not save the rookie from a long and painful trial period.

Is there any magical correct answer that can spare a rookie painful lessons in telling the truth or enduring a long initiation? Yes there is, but he is unlikely to know it unless he is a grypsman already. And he cannot figure it out. It is: "Ask other grypsmen." He does not answer "yes" or "no," but refers the inquirer to the common knowledge shared by his peers! His answer confidently asserts that other grypsmen know him, that he has acquired the right reputation, and that it can be verified by every suspicious spirit who would bother to check.

Let's assume then that a rookie knows the correct answer. Few rookies are so lucky. So why does not the rookie try to mimic a grypsman with this answer? Well, it could be the mistake of his life, a much more serious offense against the grypsmen's code than an innocent "yes." Providing the correct answer is a necessary, not a sufficient condition for a new entrant to be recognized as a grypsman. From now on, the vocabulary he uses and the way he conducts himself are closely scrutinized. He cannot imitate a grypsman by frequent cursing or playing the tough guy. Some curses are allowed, others are forbidden, and yet others are considered offensive unless "neutralized" with the proper "extension." Without this arcane knowledge, he will inadvertently start offending everybody around him. He will go down in the prison hierarchy like a stone in a pond.

The same fundamental question "are-you-a-grypsman?" may be asked in a variety of ways, sometimes without words. When a rookie enters a new cell, somebody may throw a *dish-towel* under his feet. Under no circumstances should he pick it up. He can walk over it. Better yet, he can carefully wipe his feet on it as if it were a doormat.

But what if he is not a grypsman but he knows all of these rules and all of the proper answers? Perhaps he learned them in another prison and later became a sucker after breaking a norm. Now he has been transferred to a new prison. Maybe this is the right time to start a new life?

Mimicking a grypsman is the most dangerous action one can undertake. The later a mimicker is deciphered, the harsher the punishment he faces. A newcomer grypsman is always subject to secret background checking. One or more reputable grypsmen from his previous location have to confirm that he was a grypsman. *Grypses*—secret messages—travel around the prison and between prisons in order to receive such verification. If he is coming from a distant place, background checks take longer. The system is efficient and a lie can buy him at most a few weeks. Once discovered, it leads to inevitable punishment. At the very least, he gets a severe beating and is assigned to the proper caste. In the worst-case scenario, he will be ritually raped by the fellow-grypsmen in his cell. True grypsmen have strong incentives to enforce the rules. If they fail to punish a mimicker, grypsmen from the entire cellblock may decide to downgrade the entire cell into suckers.

Let's assume for simplicity that the cell majority are grypsmen and that only four main types may enter the cell. One may be a typical *rookie* who wants to become a grypsman and who knows that lying about one's caste membership is a bad idea. One may be

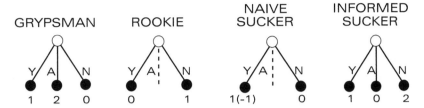

Figure 1.1. Are you a grypsman? Four decision problems.

Note: Y = Yes; A = Ask other grypsmen; N = no. The Rookie and the Naive Sucker are unaware of the third strategy, which is represented by a dotted line. The Naive Sucker incorrectly believes that the payoff for "yes" is 1, while the true payoff, represented in the parentheses, is −1.

a *naive sucker* who understands the painful consequences of being assigned to a lower caste and believes that lying can elevate him to a higher caste in the new cell. Finally, one may be a *grypsman* or an *informed sucker*, who knows the third, correct and secret, answer and assumes that lying will be inevitably detected. Figure 1.1 represents the four different decision problems that various types of newcomers face and the payoffs they attribute to particular answers.

Figure 1.1 presents the decision problem from the entrant's perspective. A rookie, grypsman, and informed sucker believe that telling the truth brings a higher payoff than lying. A naive sucker believes, incorrectly, that the best answer is "yes." A rookie and naive sucker are not aware of the correct answer.

The grypsman asking the "are-you-a-grypsman" question sees things slightly differently than they are represented in Figure 1.1. First, he is unaware which type entered the cell. Second, he knows that a rookie and naive sucker are unaware of the right answer, that an informed sucker has little incentive to take the risk of mimicking, and that only a grypsman has the incentives and knowledge to give the correct answer. He also knows that the correct payoff for a sucker answering "yes" is −1 rather than 1.

What is remarkable is that the inquirer can distinguish a grypsman from all other types. A rookie can be separated from an informed sucker with one more simple question or with a glance at his jail sentencing documents. For no type of newcomers is "yes" the most preferred answer!

The actual entry into a new cell is even more complex than I have described. A newcomer's identity is unknown, but so is the inquirer's. There are cells where the suckers rule and a grypsman may be tempted to lie in such a cell—if he guesses the identity of the cell's dwellers correctly. While most suckers reveal the truth, ensigns—entrepreneurial spirits who are willing to lie—do exist. Mimicking a grypsman is infrequent, involves a lot of risk, but it does happen. An ensign poses the highest threat to the cell's grypsmen since interacting with him may jeopardize other grypsmen's honor. The existence of ensigns provides incentives for grypsmen to maintain careful examinations, stringent background checks within and between prisons, and a strict enforcement of sanctions for lying. In this complex game the vast majority of entrants choose to tell the truth.

Welcome to the world of grypsmen. This jail is not about working out, reading, or studying foreign languages. Neither do barbarian interrogators arrive to torture inmates. The prison personnel and police are bored bureaucrats, quite ordinary people. The regime they work for is not excessively cruel. It is vastly inefficient, however, and unable to control its pariahs. It throws them into dungeons and then effectively forgets them. And the damned souls, left alone, take over the underworld and set their own rules. Doing one's time in this particular human hell is an endless, ruthless game where one may be thrown without warning into an inferior circle by one's peers. Everybody strives to figure out whom he can trust, fear, cheat, or take advantage of. Everybody hides his own dirty secrets, plays entangled games, and works out complex strategies. The reward may be the saving of his life or simply a spoon of jam. There is no escape or safe haven. A newcomer may learn the rules and face the challenge or enter a free fall into lower and lower depths.

CHAPTER TWO

The Constraints of Prison Life:

An Overview

"Lock 'em up and throw away the key." This wish is frequently repeated by Polish prison guards, nurses, policemen, and prosecutors. In fact, it is a pretty fair description of the way Polish jail is organized. One could add "cram 'em in till the last square inch is full and let 'em kill each other" and the description would be complete. Weak administrative control, scarcity of space, and the strong subculture of grypsmen are the most salient features of Polish jails. Inmates are crammed into cells, left to themselves, and subject to their own codes. They are locked in and the key is effectively thrown away. Ultimately, these factors frame the games that Polish prisoners play.

Our odyssey through the worlds of a Polish jail begins with a brief overview of its most prominent constraints. Jointly, they define an environment of "harsh social conditions"[1] or "pains of imprisonment"[2] to which inmates respond and adjust.

The constraints of prison life can be divided into three broad classes. The material constraints include the physical structure of the prison and the relative availability and scarcity of goods. The administrative system that specifies the prisoners' duties and organizes their time defines the administrative constraints. Finally, all of the informal rules of behavior that have evolved among inmates constitute the subculture. All of these constraints jointly determine the strategies available to inmates in their repeatable interactions and shape the inmates' expectations and payoffs.

MATERIAL CONSTRAINTS

Prisons and Jails

Enter the dungeons of Polish prisons in late communism. The number of inmates in all 202 Polish prisons and jails is estimated at just over 100,000 by official communist statistics and, more plausibly, at 200,000 by the underground Solidarity organization of penitentiary employees. The latter estimate means that there are about 500–600 inmates per 100,000 people. One in every four Polish men was, is, or will be doing time in prison.[3]

About one-third of all prisoners in Poland inhabit a jail. Jails host inmates awaiting trial, while those already convicted are placed in prisons. Although the official name of a jail inmate is "temporarily arrested" rather than "prisoner," he may well spend most of his sentence in a jail. Among the inmates that I met, the record was held by an inmate who was "temporarily arrested" for 4.5 years. In Poland, jails and prisons are partially separated and differ in their definitions of inmates' rights and duties. Most noticeably, jail inmates are separated more strictly to prevent the exchange of information with their alleged partners in crime. They are also rarely permitted to work or study. Thus, inmates in jail spend more time inside their cells than those in prison. Working or learning connects prisoners to the outside world, softens deprivation, helps to organize their time, and broadens their access to goods. Jail interactions are more intense than the diluted life of a convict. For a jail inmate, there is also more at stake. The length of his sentence, or perhaps even his release from jail, may depend strongly on the actions he takes during the interrogation and trial, and on his ability to recognize a potential squealer in his cell or effectively fake an illness.

Despite some of these differences, jail and prison share many characteristics. For example, convicts and temporarily arrested inmates sometimes live in the same cell. There is also no distinction between the two categories in prison hospitals. Throughout the book, I take care to mention any significant differences between prison and jail behavior or rules.

The typical prison is comprised of three- to four-floor cellblocks each hosting thirty to one hundred cells as well as visiting rooms, storage and walking areas. The cellblocks are behind a 5–6-meter high wall. Specialized units supply basic goods and services to the prison community. The main units are a laundry, sewing facilities, a kitchen, a local radio station, and a library. Given that a Polish prison menu is based on bread, there may also be a bakery. The prison's territory may also host a school, a manufacturing plant, or a hospital.

Rakowiecka, where I spent most of my five-month tenure in 1985, was among the biggest jails in the country. It consisted of three regular cellblocks and one cellblock for major political or otherwise prominent prisoners. All basic service units, press facilities, and about fifteen walking areas were located on the prison territory. A hospital cellblock included surgical, internal medicine, and psychiatric divisions. About 200 cells hosted approximately 1,800 inmates. Less than a hundred of them were women. The Siedlce prison, where the illustrator Mirek Andrzejewski spent his time as a political prisoner, was organized similarly. It was also of a similar size (see figure 2.1).

Space

Probably the most salient feature of Polish prisons is the severe lack of personal space. A typical cell in the relatively modern and well-equipped Rakowiecka and Bialoleka prisons is small. With an area of 8–14.5 m^2 and a height of about 2.5 m, it is inhabited by six to nine inmates. Large cells, called *barns*, span about 50–60 m^2 and host forty to fifty inmates. This means that there is about 1–1.5 m^2 of floor and 3–4 m^3 of air per inmate, including the space and volume consumed by the cell's furniture. Cells in jails are especially

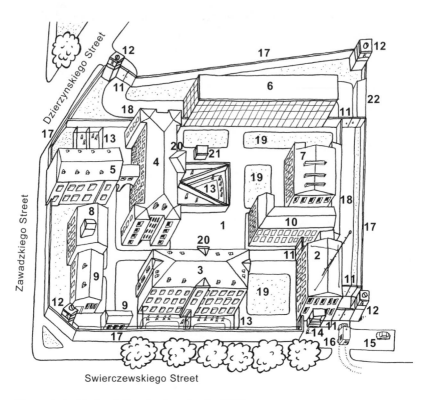

Figure 2.1. Siedlce jail and prison in the 1980s.

Note: The prison is about 150 meters wide and up to 130 long. The names of streets were changed after the fall of communism in 1989. The numbers denote: 1—Prison yard; 2—Administration (new inmates, family meetings, release and temporary release permits); 3—Prison cellblock (for convicted inmates); 4—Prison and jail cellblock (for both convicted and temporarily arrested inmates); 5—Prison hospital; 6—Prison manufacturing facility; 7—Prison school; 8—Bakery; 9—Warehouse; 10—Storage; 11—Gates; 12—Watch-towers; 13—Walkspaces; 14—Main enterance; 15—Parking for guards; 16—Prison transport van; 17—Prison walls; The Swierczewski Street wall was separated from the inside of prison by an extra net; 18—Inner roads; 19—Grass and flower-beds; 20—Entry to the cellblock for convicted inmates; 21—Well; 22—Garages. Drawing by Mirek Andrzejewski, 2003.

overcrowded. At prison hospitals, inmates enjoy two or three times as much space and volume.

One enters a cell through a massive *gate*. Usually, opposite the gate is a window that is protected by massive iron *tigerbars*. Outside the window, *blinda*—a sheet of thick translucent glass that has a

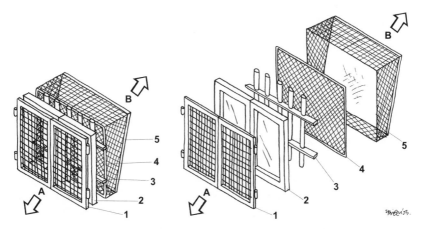

Figure 2.2. Layers of a prison window.
Note: Arrows indicate the window's orientation: A—inside cell; B—outside cell.
Numbers denote: 1— bars inside the cell; 2—window; 3—ouside bars (*tigerbars*);
4—metal net; 5—translucent glass with embedded metal net. Original prison
drawing by Mirek Andrzejewski, Siedlce prison, 1985.

metal net embedded in it—blocks the view. There may be extra
layers of nets and bars (see figure 2.2). A single dirty lightbulb in
the ceiling throws dim light on two or three grey double-decker
bunks located on the left- and right-hand sides of the cell. Grey is
the dominant color here. Blankets, clothes, walls, gate, cell floor,
cellblock halls are all grey. The narrow corridor separating the
bunks, called after the main street in Warsaw, *Marszałkowska*, hosts
most of the cell activity.[4] The furniture consists of a wooden table,
three or four stools, and a hanging shelf. *Hays*, the mattresses of
those unlucky ones who do not have their own beds, are hidden
under the bunks. One of the corners near the gate hosts a toilet
and a sink. A toilet curtain is a touch of luxury.

The toilet bowl, a prominent object in a cell, is called *jaruzel*.
The name immortalizes General Jaruzelski, who was the chairman
of the Polish communist party in 1985. A regular jaruzel and running water are high-tech equipment in cells. Many Polish prisons
lack sewage systems and instead offer a portable vessel, often called
wojtek, after General Jaruzelski's first name, or simply *general*.

Another important object in a cell is an Orwellian speaker, called
a *pneumatic drill* that is fixed over the gate and emits mostly noisy

music. The drill starts at 6:00 A.M. and stops at 9:00 P.M., with a four-hour pause around noon. When it's on, the drill randomizes between radio programs, communist rehabilitation newspeak, and a perverse mixture of hits. David Bowie's "This Is Not America" or the titles of Polish songs "A Piece of Blue Sky Is All I Need" and "How Good It Feels to Get Up at Dawn" give a fair idea of the selection algorithm. Near the speaker, by the gate, there is an emergency button that inmates can use to call a guard. It is rarely used.

An inmate may dream about a regular cell when he serves a two-week solitary confinement. Under normal circumstances, this is the harshest punishment the administration can inflict. Isolation cells are smaller and even more spartan than the regular ones. The furniture in such cells consists of the *hardbed*, that is, a block of concrete that serves as a bed, wooden boards imitating a mattress and pillow, and a concrete table and stool. All pieces of furniture are fixed to the floor. A massive pipe sticks out of the floor instead of the jaruzel. No drill, no running water, no light, no walk, few personal belongings. In select prisons, there are even harsher cells. An arrogant inmate may be taken for a weekend of beating in a *thermos*, a soundproof cell, or get immobilized in *belts*, on a bed equipped with a set of belts. After a couple of hours in belts, he loses control over urination and defecation. Soon thereafter he loses consciousness.

Spatial constraints require the careful control of one's moves and the optimal use of vertical and horizontal dimensions (see figures 2.3 and 2.4). In most cells, informal rules govern the use of space and the movement patterns of prisoners. Vertical movements down the bunks must be pre-announced: *shift*! Horizontal movement is a luxury. Often, inmates go for a "walk" inside the cell. Their walk is usually limited to a sequence of three steps, turn, three steps, turn. An odd number of steps saves inmates from vertigo that quickly comes with four-step walks. With an even number of steps, one has to make turns in the same, left or right, direction. In larger cells, it is possible to make five or even seven steps. In order to use space more efficiently, prisoners often walk in pairs or larger groups and with a high level of movement coordination.

Inmates' behavior reflects space scarcity in a variety of ways. Activities that pollute air in the cell, like passing gas or defecating, are

Figure 2.3. A bird's-eye view of a cell in Siedlce prison. Original prison drawing by Mirek Andrzejewski, Siedlce prison, 1985.

regulated and coordinated among its dwellers. Thus, the intention of passing gas must be loudly announced and one can indulge one-self only after making sure that nobody is eating. The lack of fresh air causes permanent headaches. Sedative drugs dissolved gener-ously in drinks and food by administration mitigate claustrophobia.

Goods and Food

In the spartan surroundings of a Polish prison physical objects and personal possessions are in short supply. An inmate receives prison underwear, boots, hat, shirt, linen, towels, blanket, two aluminum plates, an aluminum mug, and a spoon. The spoon's edge is quickly converted into an improvised dull knife. An inmate is allowed to

Figure 2.4. A cell in Siedlce prison. This is the same cell as in Figure 2.3 projected onto the walls. Original prison drawing by Mirek Andrzejewski, Siedlce prison, 1985.

keep his pants, socks, toilet necessities, and sometimes shoes. For a sweater or other larger items, he needs special permission. He may keep a few books, official and personal correspondence, stationery, and a small reserve of food. Other personal belongings, including the least useful object, his watch, are stored until he leaves the prison.

An inmate is not allowed to hold money except in his prison account. Twice a month, he can buy cigarettes, matches, sugar, salt, synthetic honey, poultry pâté, toothpaste, pens, stationery and other basic goods through the prison supply system—if they are available, of course! The amount one can spend is limited: the total biweekly budget buys about 400 filterless cigarettes called "Sport." The prisoner's family, if he has one, can hardly afford to feed his account with money. More often, he gets food *rockets*, or parcels. Clothes or fruit-vegetable rockets are granted as rewards by the rehabilitation personnel. Since a typical jail inmate is not permitted to work and does not earn any income himself, he rarely has anything in his account to use.

The prisoners make multiple and creative uses of the limited number of available objects. Bread, plastic bags, cardboard and paper, wood shavings, newspapers, small tin cans, towels, pen cartridges, and the like are valued. These and other items are converted into dice, playing cards, toys, simple utensils, oil lamps, tattoo equipment, portable water heaters, and even electric skillets. Illegal trade flourishes. The most valuable goods are tea, razor blades, cigarettes, and knives. Except for cigarettes, the possession of all these goods by inmates was officially forbidden in 1985.

An inmate is entitled to three meals a day. The main item in his menu is a 1.3-pound loaf of white bread, presliced into inch-thick pieces. For breakfast, he gets 1.5 ounces of margarine, a pint of wheat coffee, a microscopic amount of cheese, a tablespoon of jam, or the great communist invention, synthetic honey. Synthetic honey does not look, smell, or taste like honey. Breakfast may also consist of two pints of cereal. For dinner, served at the time of American lunch, he gets two pints of thin soup or, more often, potatoes with meat sauce and beet. The last meal is supper. The difference between supper and breakfast is that cereal is rarely served for supper.

At the end of March 1981, an inmate's daily food ration was valued at 17.30 zlotys, only slightly below a prison dog's ration valued at 18 zlotys. This amount was equivalent to just a quarter of a dollar at the black market exchange rate in 1981. A sick inmate beat the dog by a large margin, with 23.30 zlotys of food a day. His diet included, in addition to the standard menu, a pint of milk, a trace of meat, and a leaf of salad. The average daily intake of calories is officially estimated at 1,800 calories for a nonworking inmate and 2,000 calories for a working inmate.[5] The actual intake is reduced by about 10–20 percent due to theft by personnel and inmates. Food parcels from family make the most appetizing fraction of an inmate's menu.

ADMINISTRATIVE CONSTRAINTS

Interactions with Personnel

In the Polish prisons of late communism, the impact of administrative supervision on life in the cells was weaker than the literature on "total institutions" suggests.[6] Due to personnel shortages and a lack of financial resources, the prison administration limits its activities. It focuses on preventing those serious injuries that may result from prisoners' games and undertakes actions that are necessary for the preservation of the institution's security. The personnel's default attitude is apathy.

The prison administration is organized into four main units: protection, rehabilitation, management, and health service. An inmate rarely interacts with the management and only sporadically visits a doctor. Only if he is lucky does he manage to meet a dentist during his sentence. Most frequently, he interacts with prison guards from the protection unit. After the guard, the second most important personnel role in the inmate's hierarchy is a rehabilitation counselor from the rehabilitation unit, or a *rehab*.

Guards are officially addressed as *chief*, *commandant*, or *mister block-leader*. Among themselves, inmates call a guard *reptile*, *key*, *red spider*, or *bitch*. All guards are men. They escort inmates for a walk, to a doctor, or to a meeting with a family visitor. They also monitor brief morning and evening musters, assist with the distribution of food and other goods in cells, and administer *boils*—routine or punitive searches of the cell. A guard can write a report that leads to punishment. A list of the most frequent violations of rules that, if detected, result in reports includes:

- Sitting or lying on a bed between 6:00 A.M. and 6:00 P.M.
- Illegal communicating with inmates from other cells through window shouting and other means
- Stealing electricity from a lightbulb to make *czajura* (strong tea brew)
- Tattooing
- Possessing forbidden objects, such as a knife, a razor, equipment for tattooing or tea brewing, money, etc
- Bringing into or taking from a cell forbidden objects or grypses
- Making frivolous visits to a doctor
- Displaying arrogant behavior or refusing to obey personnel's orders
- Committing or attempting self-injury or helping other inmates with self-injury.

A rehab, usually a man, is supposed to work on an inmate's rehabilitation. However, with an average of one hundred or more dependents under supervision, a rehab limits his activity to visiting cells once a month, meeting new inmates and handling paperwork. An inmate can also request a meeting with him once a week. The most important part of a rehab's activity is handing out rewards or punishment, a power he shares to some extent with guards and the warden. The most frequent punishments in jail include the hardbed in an isolation cell, or the withdrawal of walking privileges and the ability to shop, meet family, borrow books, and receive parcels. Infrequently, punishment may include having one's food rations cut. A reward may suspend a punishment or provide a voucher for extra supply parcels from the family.

When inmates decide to contact other personnel about matters that they regard as important, they write to the warden, the prosecutor, or the investigator. A typical petition asks for an extra voucher, an extra family visit, or the suspension of temporary arrest. A typical response informs the inmate that no reasons were found that could justify a positive answer to his request.

Other kinds of interactions with personnel are rare, especially in jail. The warden or deputy warden visits cells once every couple of months. From time to time, a prisoner is examined by a doctor or nurse. Human rights are not enforced since all active human-rights activists are themselves imprisoned.

Time

A typical daily schedule of a nonworking jail inmate is organized as follows:

6:00 A.M.: Wake-up bell. Light is turned on briefly. The driller starts drilling. After a few minutes, inmates get back their clothes that were folded into a *cube* the day before and placed outside the cell by the gate.

6:20 A.M.: Morning muster. Inmates form a row and a cell leader— no real power attached to this function—reports to the guard any extraordinary events that took place since the previous evening's muster. Inmates use the toilet, wash, and make beds according to local regulations.

Between 7:00 and 8:00 A.M.: Breakfast. Inmates servicing cells, called *corridormen*, bring the *Titanic*—the food cart—with coffee, margarine, jam, or cheap cheese. Inmates form a line and get their portions through the open gate or a *feeder*, a small valve in the gate.

Between breakfast and dinner: Walk. It lasts about 20–25 minutes per group. Inmates walk in groups of ten to forty around one of the *walkplaces*, a 50–100 m^2 square yard. Sitting is prohibited. Smooth movement in pairs must be sustained. The 5–6 m tall wall surrounding the walkplace is covered with vagina-motivated prison prose, poetry, and paintings, quickly sketched when the bored guard is not paying attention.

11:00 A.M.: The driller pauses.

Between 12:00 and 2:00 P.M.: Dinner. After dinner, inmates get medications, bread for supper and next day's breakfast and, possibly, a communist newspaper *The People's Tribune*.

3:00 P.M.: The driller gets back to work.

Between 4:00 and 6:00 P.M.: Supper. Light is turned on again for a couple of hours until 8:30.

Between 6:00 and 6:30 P.M.: Evening muster and folding the cubes. Sitting on or lying in beds is permitted.

9:00 P.M.: Go-to-bed bell. The driller is turned off.

Weekly events include taking a shower accompanied by an exchange of underwear, one or two visits from a barber (no razors are permitted in cells), and an opportunity to visit a doctor. During a lucky week, a corridor librarian may offer 1951 novels about such stirring subjects as American industrial spies who attempted to sabotage a communist foundry, or a primer on Marxist philosophy. Once a week, inmates get hot water and cleaners to clean their cell. In some prisons, they can attend Sunday Catholic mass. Miraculously, all inmates are pious folk and never skip a mass. In jail, mass is usually broadcast by drillers.

Other events recur over larger time intervals. Inmates with money can shop in the prison store by filling out relevant forms. There are no limits on correspondence or family meetings in jail, although the meeting rights are arbitrarily granted by a prosecutor, often beginning two to three months after arresting an inmate. The average frequency of meetings depends on the family's persistence, and it is close to once a month or two months. Food rocket vouchers are distributed monthly. In prison, privileges of shopping, meeting family, writing letters, and receiving parcels are less generous than in jail. All such privileges can be suspended as punishment.

Sporadic distractions from daily routine include interrogation and trial. The most frequent of these irregular events are searches, or *boils*. Surprising by definition, cell searches are nevertheless more frequent before important holidays as well as before and after walks. Searches are also applied as a formal collective punishment for illegal cell activity that the guards were not able to attribute to a particular inmate. The goal of a search is to recover grypses, money or other illegal goods, as well as devices for tea brewing and tattooing. Many guards tacitly cooperate with benign cells and reward them by not finding such devices. Finding anything is not easy anyway since inmates are masters in the art of hiding objects in the cell and their bodies.

In *barns*, large cells, effective searches are time-consuming and difficult to organize. Guards usually limit their search activity to monitoring the degree of cell demolition with *diggers*, vertical and horizontal holes that the prisoners pierce in the walls to maintain communication and trade. When the digger's diameter passes the intervention threshold, the entire cell is transferred or taken for a long walk, and a specialized mason brigade fills the digger with concrete.

Personal searches take place before or after an inmate's family meeting, interrogation, or court visit. Infrequent collective personal searches usually go down to a careful examination of inmates' clothes and their body cavities. Inmates must undress completely in the hall and stand naked by the wall with their arms raised and legs spread wide apart.

The personnel do not have sufficient resources to interact with the inmates intensively. Administratively organized time in jail takes about 2–4 hours out of an inmate's day. The inmates use the remaining time for their own activities. This feature of Polish prisons makes prison life relatively independent from the administration.

Thus, while space and many basic goods are scarce, unstructured time is abundant. A prisoner's private part of the day is organized around the main activity provided by the personnel, his meals. Between meals, there is plenty of time to kill. Reading is rarely a feasible solution in small cells due to the lack of light and air, and scarce sitting space. The price for long intellectual activity is severe headaches. An inmate's dream is to fall asleep one day and wake up half a year later. The abundance of time creates a market for entertainment. Singing, tattooing, story-telling, drawing, an ability to play cards or chess, and a proficiency in puzzle-solving are all highly valued skills. Reports on advances in the science of hibernation make frequent winners in story-telling contests. To *silters*, inmates who get depressed, a beating therapy is applied and such inmates often leave the cell through self-injury. Many other negative psychological or material burdens imposed on cellmates, such as unannounced farting or defecating, are punished. Discreet masturbation is usually allowed in beds after the *night alert*, or *curfew*, is announced by the inmates. Little daily routines are celebrated.

SUBCULTURAL CONSTRAINTS: A GLIMPSE AT THE WORLD OF GRYPSMEN

Excluding inmates with transitionary status, such as rookies and newbies, the community of Polish inmates is most often self-sorted into three separate castes: *grypsmen*, *suckers*, and *fags*. The inclusion of a prisoner in one of these three categories usually takes place shortly after arrest. Grypsmen were most numerous in the Bialoleka and Rakowiecka prisons. According to my estimates, about 70–80 percent of all inmates were in this group. The proportion of grypsmen in most other jails is similar. In prisons, the proportion of grypsmen is typically lower.

Almost any new prisoner may become a member of the grypsing group. The norms of this group, which to a great extent regulate the patterns of inmate behavior through a set of rules, prohibitions, and customs, are the core elements of the prison subculture. There are five "codified" *principles* of grypsing, in which inmates are enjoined to (a) show solidarity with other prisoners, (b) exhibit noncooperation with the prison administration, (c) help weaker inmates, (d) uphold the grypsmen's honor code, and (e) observe strict personal hygiene. These rules are open to interpretation and differ in details from one prison to another, but most importantly, their application is limited only to grypsmen and not to suckers or fags.

Grypsmen speak a secret language, which is bound by complicated regulations. Specific meanings are placed on certain words, in particular those that are generally used when addressing women. To compare a grypsman to a woman, communist, collaborator, or a fag, or the mere suggestion of such a comparison, is the greatest possible insult.

To become a grypsman, an eligible inmate has to memorize all the principles and other rules. This process is similar to learning the common law through "case study." At the first stage, an inmate must pass a series of tests of his intellectual ability, strength of character, and resistance to pain. In some cells, he is subject to a ritual of *baptism*. At the end of his education, the inmate must acquire fluency in the secret argot and norms.

Suckers, a less numerous and atomized group, occupy darker corners of the cell. Frightened and exploited by grypsmen, they clean the cell and perform various services for the higher caste. A grypsman cannot shake a sucker's hand or eat with him at a table. However, he can steal from him. Suckers are considered actual or potential informers. A grypsman can become a sucker as a result of committing an *offense*. Almost all nongrypsmen are suckers since the last group, *fags*, makes up only 1–2 percent of the jail population.

A fag is a male prostitute who once agreed to sexually please a grypsmen or, less often, was raped or otherwise sexually humiliated. Sometimes a fag is not active sexually but his stigma is nonremovable anyway. He is given a feminine name and occupies the small toilet territory around the jaruzel. The jaruzel's seat is his table. A grypsman assumes that every fag is a potential informer. Thus, norms of grypsing forbid him from virtually all interactions with a fag, except one—to "fuck" him. A grypsman is allowed to assume the active role in a homosexual intercourse, while a fag's role must be passive.

Strict rules govern vertical mobility among the castes. A grypsman who seriously violates the group's norms may become a sucker. Another grypsman ceremonially calls a curse down on him and makes him a sucker or, in most serious cases, a fag. A sucker may move up in the hierarchy, but it is pretty difficult. In such a case, the necessary condition is that the curse-holder withdraw the curse.

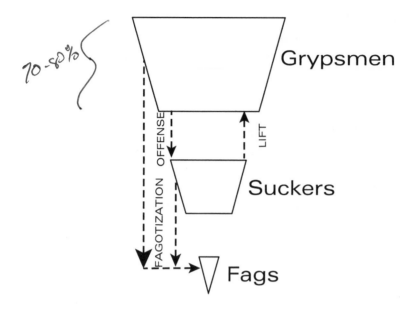

70-80%

Figure 2.5. Relations among major castes. The areas of the polygons represent approximately the relative size of each caste at the Bialoleka and Rakowiecka jails. Vertical arrows show the possible directions of intercaste mobility.

Often, a sucker who is waiting for a *lift* is encouraged to support his application with generous gifts. *Fagotization*, or becoming a fag, is irreversible and often follows a failed test of *fag-making*. Thus, the labels are "sticky" and it is difficult or even impossible to upgrade to a higher caste (see figure 2.5).[7]

In various prisons, other ephemeral castes emerged, often incubated by occasional and moderately successful attempts by the personnel at social engineering. Among them, *fests* or *ladybugs* exhibited the organization and norms similar to grypsmen, while *Swiss* pretended to be neutral in intergroup conflicts. The existence of new castes, or the relative size of grypsmen and suckers' castes, strongly influence intergroup social relations.[8]

There is some differentiation in status and power within the highest caste. In most cells, a core of the ruling inmate elite called *elders* emerges. They initiate character tests that are applied to rookies, impose their interpretation of the tests' results in cases of doubt, and explore profits from conflict arbitration. However, strong norms of intragrypsmen brotherhood prevent deeper inequities. A powerless and helpless grypsman must first be converted into a sucker before being systematically exploited by his peers.

NOTE ON IMPORTATION VERSUS DEPRIVATION

Sociological observers of American prisons have long noted that, in addition to prison-specific *deprivation*, incarcerated individuals *import* certain dispositions and patterns of behavior when they arrive at the prison and continue to exhibit them while behind bars. For example, American prisons are violent places in considerable part because violence is imported into them.[9] Thus, one of the central questions of prison studies is whether the norms of prison subculture are imported from the outside world or whether they arise as a response to the "pains" of imprisonment.

Anecdotal evidence about norms regulating defecation and passing gas, the coordination of individual movement, and the ingenious techniques for producing simple goods supports the importance of deprivation. There is also a strong correlation between the level of control exerted in cells, cellblocks, or prisons and the strength of inmate subculture. On the other hand, some evidence points to the importance of importation. The presence of political prisoners, who bring dramatically different patterns of behavior that they usually stick to, typically softens the harsh grypsmen norms and reduces conflict. One may conjecture that the elitist and narrow subculture of thieves which gave birth to the universal subculture of grypsmen was in part due to the political thaw of 1956 that suddenly halted the inflow of political prisoners.

Inmate interactions are reconstructed in this book without controlling for the social characteristics of the entrant population. Such characteristics are taken as given. In general, this book is less concerned with assessing the relative impact of deprivation versus importation on the subculture than with the reconstruction of particular customs, norms, and typical interactions.

CHAPTER THREE

Becoming a Grypsman

INITIATION TESTS

Initiation rituals welcome newcomers to most human communities. Entering a total institution with a strong subculture can be especially traumatic.[1] A newcomer may face trials of his acumen, tolerance for pain, self-confidence, alertness, physical strength and endurance, or sense of humor. After passing various tests, often humiliating or otherwise unpleasant, he is expected to learn local norms and customs quickly. When he carelessly abuses a norm, a mild or harsh punishment teaches him the proper behavior. Finally, the group assigns him a label that "compresses the variegated range of [the group's] experience into a manageable framework."[2] This learning process runs parallel to the training in the institution's formal code and is tolerated, if not encouraged, by the personnel. The entire experience of rapid socialization to a new environment transforms a rookie into a fully adapted inmate.

When a new entrant to the cell in a Polish jail answers the fundamental "are-you-a-grypsman?" question, the complex process of allocating him to the proper caste begins. A *newbie*, a newcomer to a cell who already belongs to one of the three castes, settles quickly.

The background checking is usually completed within a few hours and his declaration is authenticated. For a rookie, the path to his final destiny is usually longer and takes from a few weeks to a few months. Almost every rookie declares the desire to join the grypsmen and almost everybody is eligible for that honor. Exceptions include child molesters, junkies, members of the communist party, or functionaries of the penal or law enforcement systems, such as prison guards, judges, prosecutors, and policemen. Criminal lawyers are welcome. A rookie joins the caste after completing a long series of *initiation tests*. Often, he is not aware that his actions and words are under scrutiny. His status at this stage is similar to that of a sucker.

In Polish jails, two initial tests include fag-making and baptism. Fag-making provides a first screening for rookies who seem unfit for caste membership. Baptism is a ceremony most popular in large cells. The stage of "little games" and "hidden tests" provides a comprehensive assessment of a rookie's potential strengths and weaknesses. When the cell's rulers consider the performance exceptionally strong, the rookie quickly advances to the final phase. If this is not the case, new tests are continuously applied. The final stage provides a rookie with intensive training in secret argot and language games, the code of behavior, and the meaning of various games from the previous stage. A masterful command of this body of knowledge is a prerequisite for full caste membership (see figure 3.1).

Tests are performed and developed by the old inmates and provide them with multiple benefits. Often affected by emotional and sensual deprivation, inmates enjoy tests immensely. They can take revenge on a rookie for their own humiliation or suffering. Clear-cut lines between "new" and "old" inmates elevate the latter to a higher strata in the local social structure. Although denying selfish reasons, the test designers may be motivated by valuable goods brought by the newcomer. The one controlling the tests' results sometimes receives a portion of the rookie's endowment. Finally, as a by-product, a compressed initiation experience helps the rookie to adjust mentally to the new environment. Such accelerated "prisonization" benefits the old inmates as well.[3] It prevents the new-

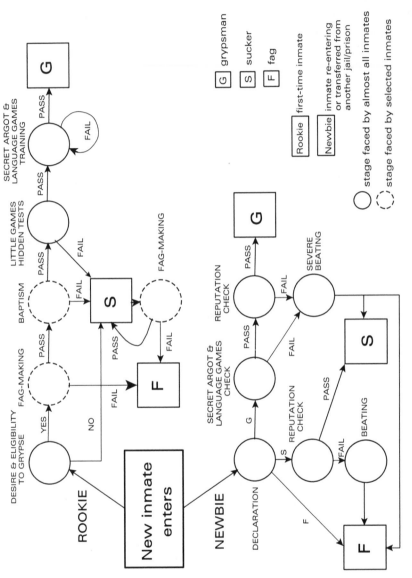

Figure 3.1. Stage diagram for allocation of new inmates among castes. At the first stage, rookies are separated from newbies. A rookie is subject both to testing and learning. A newbie is subject only to a verification of his initial declaration. A grypsman may fall into a lower caste after he commits a serious offense against the norms of grypsing.

comer from looking back, lamenting what he sees now as a lost paradise, and tormenting the fragile peace of mind of his better adapted fellow inmates.

This list of benefits is incomplete. In Polish prisons the main objective of the initiation rituals, according to the inmates' common knowledge, is to collect detailed information about the rookie's *character* or *type*. *Toughness* and *cleverness* are two of the primary characteristics of an inmate. Old inmates who learn about these characteristics of the rookie form clearer expectations about his future behavior. This allows them to optimally exploit the rookie's skills and take advantage of his weaknesses. In addition, toughness serves as a proxy for the rookie's expected loyalty in conflicts with the personnel.

The incentives to uncover a rookie's true type are especially strong when cellblocks are isolated, when the control of prison personnel is weak, and when inmates change cells frequently. Usually, it is in the rookie's best interest to convince the old inmates that he is both tough and smart. Only occasionally may he find it more valuable to be labeled *unpredictable* or *broken*.[4]

FIRST SCREENING: FAG-MAKING AND BAPTISM

A young, physically and intellectually weak rookie may face various "first-screening" tests. A failure in such a test prevents him from joining the grypsmen caste. Whether he will be a sucker or a fag depends on the magnitude of the failure.

Fag-making is a fundamental test of toughness. Victims of this test typically report violent rape. The evidence I collected suggests that a violent rape takes place less often than is reported, and that many victims misreport what actually happened. The "rape" often denotes a victim's consent to perform passive homosexual service in exchange for protection and other benefits. Such an interpretation is often presented by those who *avoided* rape.[5]

The test is preceded by intensive repressions. Passing unexpected flatulence in the rookie's face, stealing, nudging, rationing food, and speculating on the details of the rookie and his family's sexual life may fill the entire critical day. The rookie is told that he must face such oppressions for a long period of time before he can be admitted as a grypsman. Then, in the night, one of the executioners leans toward his bed with the offer, "You, you do not be afraid. I tell the boys, they leave you alone. You get your bed back and they let you defecate on the throne at will. But do something for me. Suck my cock. Only once. They will never know. You do it and you are free forever."[6]

A deceived rookie who accepts the offer becomes a fag, receives a feminine name, and must eat and live near the throne. In some cases he is periodically raped. More often, he gets used to the new role and performs sexual services voluntarily.

The strategic context of the test explains why actual and potential victims might describe it differently, and what their incentives are for doing so. It is unlikely that those who fail will learn that they *did not* have to accept the offer since, as fags, they will be informationally isolated in the cell. Conversely, those who pass the test will soon learn that fag-making is a test and that there are standard procedures for conducting such a test. Moreover, the decision to submit to pressure always involves an estimate of the feasibility and desirability of further resistance. Resistance may be thought of as "impossible" and "life-threatening" or one can decide to "fight till death." One of these two representations appears in virtually all descriptions of attempted prison rape. In fact, the test's presumed objective is precisely to create an artificial situation in which the subject forms such a mental representation, and to separate weak (those who surrender) from tough subjects (those who decide to fight).

Baptism is common in large cells, called *barns*. Those who fail become suckers, not fags. In forty to fifty-person barns, there is a constant inflow of five to ten new inmates per month. Once every couple of weeks, a "painful" and "bloody" ritual is prepared by the elders to examine the rookies' immunity to pain. Cruel tales of rookies losing their limbs or life fill the waiting period. Forget the pain, say the elders, every true grypsman must pass the test. Those who fail do not deserve the privilege of joining the caste. Those who survive become grypsmen.

Deep into the night, in the light of torches made of butter and sheets, rookies are blindfolded and spread on the stools. The *butcher*, inmate-executioner, prepares a special wet towel that is supposed to "break the rookie's bones" and yet not leave external signs of beating. Surrounded by a circle of blood-thirsty half-naked inmates, the rookie awaits mortal blows. As the slaughter is about to begin, the butcher offers him an option out of the ceremony in exchange for forgoing grypsmen membership. Those who accept, frightened by the performance, immediately get cursed and beaten by the butcher. They become suckers.

Those who resist the temptation to opt out become eligible for the next stage of initiation. The actual blows paid by the butcher are symbolic. In fact, baptism is a harmless spectacle. Severe beating, as promised by the terrifying setup, may be met with disciplinary action and extra sentences for those involved. Thus, a harsh test is costly to implement for the elders. Since the supply of uninformed rookies in jails is steady, there is no need to use random beatings or other devices to enhance credibility.[7]

Since there are several rookies and the test is conducted sequentially, the decision of a particular rookie to face the test reveals the truth to those waiting in line. This creates inequity among rookies: if a rookie fails, then all his successors preserve the chance of passing; if he passes, then all his successors pass. This property of the test motivates the elders to manipulate the waiting line. Experienced elders often begin with the rookies who are most likely to fail or otherwise arrange the line according to their interests by placing their favorite rookies at the end.

The games of fag-making and baptism exploit fundamental knowledge asymmetries between old inmates and rookies about basic prison customs, norms, and argot. The structure of both tests is similar. The rookie faces a simple binary decision: he may accept an offer by an elder (A), or reject it (R). The decision problem is constructed as a choice between performing some humiliating activity or cowardly defection versus a ritualized beating or some other form of repression. This choice is supposed to open the gates to joining the grypsmen caste. If a rookie chooses A, he expects

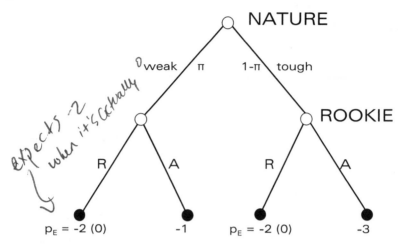

expects -2 when it's actually 0

Figure 3.2. Generic screening test.
Note: *A*—accept; *R*—reject. Term p_E is the adjustment for the expected pain; Rookie's estimate is $p_E = -2$; Test designer's private knowledge: $p_E = 0$. When $p_E = -2$, a tough Rookie chooses *R* while a weak Rookie chooses *A*.

that his honor suffers; if he chooses *R*, he expects physical and psychological suffering (see figure 3.2).

The declared goal behind this test is to distinguish between tough and weak rookies. A weak rookie does not care enough about his honor and prefers *A* rather than face the painful consequences of *R*. A tough rookie is supposed to "value his honor above life" and prefer *R* to *A*. Thus, the rookie's choice reveals his type.

However, the catch in the game is that a rookie is misled by the elders. He overestimates the value of the term p_E (the future physical pain from choosing *R*), compared to the payoffs related to the loss of honor. The actual value of p_E, which is the elders' private knowledge, is zero and makes the rejection of the offer a better choice for both types. Misrepresenting p_E rather than performing the test as expected decreases the number of violent interactions in a cell and the subsequent exposure of the elders to punishment from the personnel.

Both tests suffer from a certain flaw. Student, who was the subject of fag-making in the version described earlier, did not have to be tough to choose the better option. He was able to figure out that

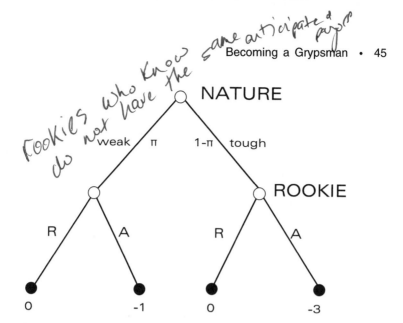

rookies who know the same anticipated payoff do not have the

Figure 3.3. Generic screening test with informed rookie.
Note: *A*—accept; *R*—reject. The informed Rookie knows that there is no pain adjustment affecting his payoffs. *R* is a trivial dominant strategy for the Rookie.

he faced a toughness test and that refusal dominated acceptance. The declared purpose of the test, to check whether he was tough or weak, remained unfulfilled.

The flaw is that the tests work only for an uninformed rookie, in other words, a rookie who believes in the masquerade. For an informed rookie, the test is inconclusive since refusal is a better choice for both types (see figure 3.3).

Games from figures 3.2 and 3.3 can be combined into a larger four-type game, that is, a game with an informed-uninformed dimension in addition to a tough-weak dimension. It is clear that in such a game the test designer can identify an uninformed weak rookie but is unable to distinguish between a truly tough rookie and a weak informed rookie. The rookie may be informed because he is "smart" or because he got a hint from somebody else. Although the consequences of distributing such hints can be painful, such indiscretions happen and nullify the type-revealing value of the test. However, grypsmen monitor themselves quite closely and effectively prevent major leaks or the sloppy performance of test executioners.

A test designer may himself be a guinea pig in a larger game. After a while spent in jail, Student learned that Maniek, his potential rapist, was himself subject to a test. Maniek's task was to make a fag of a rookie. His performance was not stellar since Student figured out the hidden purpose of his proposal. Maniek flunked his higher-level test, though his punishment was merely to not advance his status among the other inmates.

LITTLE GAMES

Once a rookie is accepted as a candidate for grypsing, perhaps after optional stages of fag-making and/or baptism, he is subjected to a series of lighter and more sophisticated tests that primarily target his cleverness and, less frequently, toughness.[8] The interim period of observation and tests is called *America* and lasts from a few weeks to a few months. The name "America" reflects both the traumatic experience of Polish immigrants in a new society and the wry sense of prison humor, juxtaposing the promised land with a rookie's miserable status. America in Polish prisons is a more important component of prisonization than the personnel-enforced socialization to the new environment.

The games or decision situations are carefully arranged, analyzed, and evaluated by the cell's elders. After each major interaction they decide whether to let the rookie join the grypsmen, make him a sucker, or keep testing. A candidate may be unaware that the game is being played. In *little games*, either the fact that a ritual game is being played is common knowledge or a typical rookie can figure this out during the decision-making process. On the other hand, the rookie is kept unaware of the true character of various *hidden games* that arise in a natural way during everyday interactions.

Little games take place in late evening, or at night, after the cell is closed. All grypsmen secretly prepare the scene and coordinate their efforts. The accessories include dish-towels, mugs, stools, blankets, and other equipment in the cell. Typically, more senior grypsmen try to keep low profiles that will guarantee their safety in case of an accident. The main actors are the rookie and more junior grypsmen.

Prison legends say that little games evolved from the final comprehensive exams of Polish and Russian prewar underground thief universities. One can find many games that resemble these little games in Soviet gulags.[9] Payoffs reward toughness, alertness, the readiness to act and disregard irrelevant facts. If a rookie does especially well, his America may be shortened and he quickly becomes a grypsman. Poor scores in initial trials result in a prolonged testing period and tougher, more violent, tests.

Little games resemble both social psychology experiments and artificial decision situations of experimental game theory. The declared objective is to sort the rookies into types. Other, nondeclared, benefits play an important role in providing motivation for the elders to design and implement the games. Playing games provides desirable fun and distraction. Commenting on the outcomes of past games is one of the favorite conversational topics in a cell. The designer is often rewarded for his role in the game by winning prestige and valuable prison goods that he can more or less violently extract from a rookie. All these payoffs make skills at designing tests a valuable asset for every grypsman.

The following short catalog lists a small subset of actively played little games. Many variants exist that bear different names (see figure 3.4).

> *Bicycle:* A piece of newspaper is put among a sleeping rookie's toes and lit. A rookie involuntarily starts "bicycling" with his legs and next wakes up. Expectation: alertness and loyalty.
>
> *Blindman's Bluff:* An inmate-volunteer, blindfolded with a dish-towel, tries to catch and identify one of the other inmates. They shove and nudge him. In fact, the inmate sees through the sloppily tied dish-towel. He goes after rookie, catches him, and identifies him. Next, the blindfolded rookie takes a monumental anonymous beating. Expectation: the rookie guesses the designer's intentions and oversees tying up the dish-towel on the first inmate so that he is actually blind and cannot pick anybody in particular.

Figure 3.4. Little games. Clockwise from the window: Views, Blindman's Bluff, Bicycle, Prison Car, Diver, Smells. Drawing by Mirek Andrzejewski, 2003.

Boeing Pilot: A rookie is blindfolded with a dish-towel and placed on a stool. He is told that he will be lifted to the ceiling by two grypsmen. In fact, the grypsmen only shake the stool at the floor level which creates an impression of lifting. At some point, they enlarge the amplitude of shakes and the rookie falls on a blanketed floor. His reaction is carefully watched.

Cable Car: A rookie, who is lying on the upper plank-bed level, is suddenly asked by a lower-level grypsman: "Do you have a ticket?" Answering "yes" is expected. Any other answer results in the line "Get out of my cable car, free-rider!" and a strong kick from downside which throws him out of the bed onto the floor.

Cell Leader: A rookie picks a match with his mouth. If he picks a long match, he is supposed to become a new cell leader; if he picks a short match, he loses. The rookie is blindfolded with a dish-towel. Then, some inmate instantly takes his pants down, fixes the matches in his naked buttocks, and places it under the rookie's lips. A dumb rookie kisses the bottom; a smart rookie checks the objects with a hand or loosens the dish-towel discreetly in order to monitor the course of action.

Dentist: A rookie's teeth are cleaned. When he opens his mouth and closes his eyes, the cell's ashtray content is emptied there. Expectation: do not close your eyes completely and monitor the events.

Disneyland: An arbiter immobilizes a rookie's knees between his own. He shows his right fist, this is Donald Duck, then his left fist, this is Mickey Mouse. Next, he hits the rookie right above the knee, a very painful spot, and asks "Who hit you?" Answering "Donald" or "Mickey" leads to another blow and a repetition of the question. The game ends when the expected answer is provided: "you."

Diver: A rookie stands on the bed and has to "dive" head first into a small mug of water placed on the floor. In reality, the diver is safe. While he is being blindfolded, other inmates quickly spread a protective blanket between the bunks. Toughness in the face of danger is expected.

Prison Car: The rookie is thrown under the bed while two prisoners press him to the wall with stools. The "driver" commands "Get him in first gear-second-third," causing increasing pressure. Expected response is, "Put it in neutral."

Smells: Blindfolded with a dish-towel, a rookie has to guess the identity of certain items from their smells when they are placed under his nose. He recognizes bread and margarine, and when he is ready to inhale again, someone squeezes toothpaste under his nose. Expectation: be cautious when inhaling.

Storm: A rookie, often sleeping, is bundled in a blanket and immobilized by a few grypsmen. The designer tells his story: "The storm is gathering—first thunder strikes—it starts raining—thunder storm begins." The grypsmen strike him once with an aluminum mug, throw water on him, next give him a series of strikes, etc. The expected reaction is to declare "good weather."

Views: A rookie stands in front of a window in order to see a bit of the outside world. He must describe what he sees. An answer like "car," "man," "tree," etc. results in a wet-towel blow. Expected answer is "I see freedom."

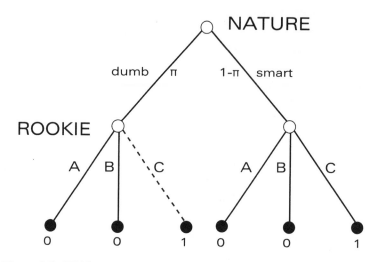

Figure 3.5. Hidden strategy test.

Note: {*A,B*}—the suggested set of answers or actions; *C*—correct (expected) answer or action. A dumb Rookie, unaware of *C*, chooses between *A* or *B* while a smart Rookie chooses *C*.

In the Bicycle, Boeing Pilot, or Diver games, grypsmen carefully monitor a rookie's reaction to a danger or an unusual situation. These games have a structure similar to Generic Screening. Unusual toughness brings extra rewards. Student's buddy, who jumped on the floor before the signal was given and the blanket was placed, hurt his neck. He reported to the doctor that he "fell from bed," and his demonstration of loyalty immediately ended his America with a positive result.

Other little games are simple decision problems similar to the Hidden Strategy Test (figure 3.5). In Disneyland, Cable Car, Prison Car, Storm, or Views, the torture ends when the rookie figures out the hidden strategy and shouts out the magic formula. The framing of such a game implicitly suggests to a rookie some set of available strategies. Outside of this set of "naive" strategies there is a "correct" answer or expected reaction. A dumb rookie chooses *A* or *B*, a strategy from an implicitly suggested set, while a smart rookie picks the expected *C*. Again, an informed rookie passes the test effortlessly.

Finally, games like Blindman's Bluff, Cell Leader, or Smells test for smart and cautious reactions. The rookie's best outcome occurs when he figures out an ingenious strategy that reverses the roles and makes fun out of the fun-maker. In Cell Leader, an informed rookie may pretend to be an uninformed one and secretly hide a needle in his mouth. When the tester's naked bottom is placed in front of him, he may prick the naked bottom painfully instead of picking matches. Such an impressive demonstration of skills ends the testing period immediately.[10]

HIDDEN TESTS

A rookie is often tested even though he does not know that his behavior is being carefully scrutinized.[11] Fag-making is the primary example of such a test. Other tests are arranged around typical situations of everyday life. In such situations, an aggressive grypsman may bully the rookie and ask him to choose between imitating a dog or a cat for everybody's fun. Somebody passes gas in the rookie's face. When the narrow corridor between the double-deck bunks is temporarily occupied by other inmates, the rookie who wants to get to the window is asked to use the under-the-bed detour. The tests have a simple structure and simple solutions. The optimal reaction is to refuse any humiliating activity and stay tough against aggression. Again, a smart reaction, like singing an anti-communist song when a song is requested, may lead to extra rewards.

Many confrontation games arise around attempts to redistribute simple prison goods. A rookie brings in a bunch of valuable items like new pants, shoes, shirts, socks, vitamins, toothpaste, food, or money. Some of these goods can be discreetly stolen and immediately transferred to another cell via the grypsmen's network. Other goods, like pants or shoes, can be extracted only via ingenious stealing at night or via a forced "exchange" for some prison junk clothes. An elder may try on the rookie's prison boots and declare that they fit him perfectly. Stealing, a forced exchange, or pushing a rookie to perform unpleasant or even humiliating services sparks a confrontation. Almost all rookies face such a confrontation in various forms many times. Those who choose correctly will score well and, as a bonus, retain their property and dignity.

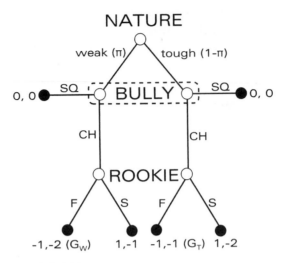

Figure 3.6. One-sided chicken.

Note: The game according to Rookie. *CH*—challenge, *F*—fight, *S*—surrender, *SQ*—status quo. Rookie's private knowledge: his type, weak or tough. Bully's private knowledge: G_T and G_W, i.e., one extra move. Rookie believes that the game ends at the nodes with G_T and G_W and estimates the expected payoffs at $E_R(G_T)$ = $(-1,-1)$ and $E_R(G_W)$ = $(-1,-2)$. Subgames G_T and G_W are shown in fig. 3.7.

Almost all games of confrontation between an old inmate and a rookie fit one clear pattern that somewhat resembles a one-sided game of *Chicken*. In Chicken, players simultaneously choose between two actions, fight (*F*) or surrender (*S*). The player's most preferred outcome is winning. The second preferred outcome is mutual surrendering which is better than losing by surrendering, which in turn is preferred to a destructive duel. In *One-Sided Chicken*, similar preferences are attributed to weak fellows who fear a physical injury and would defect against a tough opponent. Defection damages one's reputation and the prison code places great value on being tough under all circumstances. Thus, a tough rookie (player 2) prefers mutual fighting rather than surrendering.

The game begins when the *Bully* commits himself to a tough stance instead of sticking with the status quo (*SQ*). He challenges the Rookie with the first move and waits for his reaction (figure 3.6).

Rookie attributes standard "tough" preferences to his opponent, in other words, he assumes that the defense is costly since Bully is determined to fight. His reaction depends on his type. When

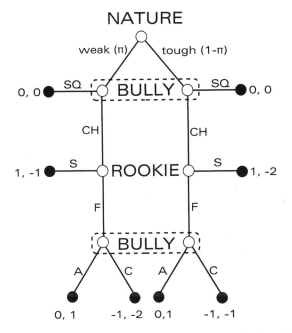

Figure 3.7. Fake chicken.
Note: The game according to Bully. *CH*—challenge, *F*—fight, *S*—surrender, *C*—continue fighting, *A*—announce that Rookie passed the test, *SQ*—status quo. Rookie's private knowledge: his type, weak or tough.

Bully initiates the fight, a weak rookie surrenders, while a tough rookie fights.

However, Rookie is unaware of the crucial fact that Bully has an extra move. One-Sided Chicken is a typical Rookie's subjective representation of the game that in fact involves additional actions. When Rookie fights, Bully can continue fighting or withdraw from the confrontation, that is, he can announce that Rookie passed the test. At that stage, action *A* dominates *C* for Bully. Thus, the game ends with a weak rookie surrendering or Bully announcing that a tough rookie passed the test. Rookie has a dominant strategy in One-Sided Chicken: weak *S*; tough *F*, while Bully has a weakly dominant strategy in the game that better describes the interaction, Fake Chicken: *CH*; *A* after Rookie's *F* (see figure 3.7).

Again, information problems obscure the diagnostic value of Fake Chicken. When Rookie is informed, when the game in Figure 3.7, which better represents the actual interaction than the game in figure 3.6, is common knowledge, there exists a trivial equilibrium in dominant or weakly dominant strategies. The equilibrium strategies are:

Bully: *CH*; *A* after Rookie's *F*.
Rookie: Always *F*.

The extra action *A* for Bully is crucial for his incentive to initiate the game. Action *A*, "announce that Rookie passed the test," can be distinguished from "surrendering" only because the actual game is common knowledge among the cell's elders. If Rookie declines to accept Bully's withdrawal, they quickly confirm that the game was a test. In fact, the elders' readiness to re-interpret the game solves the collective action problem for them of how to exploit a newcomer and not risk losing prestige or getting injured when the rookie turns out to be tough. Thus, the existence of a hidden move provides an ingenious insurance policy against tough rookies for all of the cell's elders. In the absence of effective punishments for bullying by the prison's authority, such a policy provides sufficient incentives for potential Bullies to initiate tests.

PRISON UNIVERSITY

A rookie who passes all the tests is accepted as a future grypsman.[12] The final stage of advancement is a secret training, called *bajera*, or *prison university*.[13] At this stage he should be familiar with all the basic customs and argot vocabulary. It is now expected that he will learn all the basic and secondary secret norms, the secret argot grammar that constrains argot usage, the meaning of tests, and the mechanics of sanctions and intercaste mobility.

In late night courses of prison university, a rotating team of instructors conveys the secret knowledge to the candidates. The rookies gather around the instructor on his bunk and spend two to three hours learning, reciting formulas, and answering questions. After a few days, a rookie is almost unconscious from sleeplessness. Since instructors rotate, they do not waste more than one night a week.

The instructors work *pro bono* and their feelings of pride and satisfaction from the progress of their students resemble, to some extent, the feelings of doctoral advisors. They also devote more time to smarter students. Teaching in barns, where the performance of an instructor affects to some extent his status and may be monitored by other grypsmen, appears to be of higher quality than that in smaller cells. However, instructors have strong incentives to work well in all cells. Although an instructor is not motivated by tenure or salary raises, his reputation may suffer when he lets an undereducated student pass. The loyalty of a clever and tough graduate provides him with extra protection in case of trouble.

The pressure on the rookie to learn all of the details and spirit of the secret code is very strong. A typical training consists of between fifty and one hundred hours of lectures and exams. The amount of material required to learn, including the preceding internship, could hardly be covered in fewer than two or three undergraduate courses. Thus, *grypsing studies* could constitute a minor field at an eccentric college. The body of knowledge is so vast that the initial training is supposed to cover the fundamentals only. Even toward the end of his tenure a grypsman can be exposed to a new term or be surprised by a puzzling situation.

The exam is spread out over time. The questions are repeated until all basic mistakes have been eliminated. One can be awakened by an instructor at midnight and be asked a question. Dumb rookies are eliminated at the earlier stages with fag-making, little games, or other tests, and practically all candidates have the intellectual capacity to learn the required material. Since they have strong incentives to work hard, all of them are sooner or later admitted as proper grypsmen.

The secret training empowers a grypsman to send a credible signal of his caste membership. It is his insurance policy and protective endowment when he is transferred to a new cell or a prison. It is also a proxy for all his prison skills. His wit and humor are channeled through joyful playing with the subculture's terms. No wonder that sometimes grypsmen fall deeply in love with their secret code and that a masterful command of quips and rules becomes their lifelong passion.

CHAPTER FOUR

Prison Code of Behavior

Inmates speak their own language, cultivate their own customs and rituals, and adhere to their own norms. They laugh at a joke that an external observer would find lame and react violently to an apparently friendly gesture. Their interpretation of behavior is clearly different from outside society. It is dictated by their own prison code, which categorizes behavior as hostile, offensive, neutral, or friendly in its own fashion.

A part of the prison code can easily be reconstructed from the observation of everyday interactions. Most of the vocabulary and various customs regulating simple cell activities belong to the prison public domain. Those semi-secret elements of the prison code share some properties. First, it may be practically difficult to keep some of the elements of the code secret against lower caste inmates or guards. Thus, inmates from all castes, as well as guards, name objects that they encounter and activities that they jointly undertake in the same way. Second, activities like defecation or flatulence are a potential source of negative externalities for all cell dwellers. Coordinating such activities and enforcing cooperation is beneficial for everybody. Grypsmen make little effort to keep related norms secret and often encourage lower castes to learn the rules. A smart rookie can pick up basic vocabulary in a few weeks without any training as well as learn fundamental norms and customs.

The hidden part of the code is strictly secret and much more difficult to infer from everyday interactions. It regulates less routine activities and the use of argot. Broadly defined secret rules of behavior prescribe what is proper and what is unsuitable in a variety of situations. Argot rules prohibit or demand certain combinations of words. The secret rules link publicly observable rules with more fundamental norms. Thus, the secret part of the prison code consists both of a body of secret rules and of higher-level justifications of publicly observable behavior and customs.

A rookie or a researcher would find it extremely difficult to learn the secret code from other than a well-experienced grypsman. However, a grypsman has little incentive to cooperate with a researcher. The revelation of rules to personnel or members of lower castes is severely punished by his peers. Pretending to be a prisoner through participant observation would be of little help. Grypsmen's techniques for *deciphering* a squealer—and a researcher pretending to be an inmate—are complex, ingenious, and efficient. Moreover, the interaction skills of a savvy grypsman beat those of a typical researcher by a large margin. I was deciphered *twice* by my fellow inmates as an undercover sociologist despite the fact that I was a regular inmate! My cellmates were able to guess my research intentions even though all supporting documents, relevant stories, correspondence, and psychological correlates of imprisonment were in place.

Even the "public" character of the semi-secret code does not make it readily available to a curious spectator. Grypsmen are unwilling to share any information with others unless its public character is indisputable or if it would enhance their welfare when revealed. Moreover, they do not reveal that any "secret" knowledge actually exists. Suckers who have never completed a grypsmen training, prison personnel, or naïve researchers can mistakenly assume that the semi-secret code is in fact the entire "secret prison knowledge."

THE SEMI-SECRET CODE

Semi-secret norms revolve around food, eating, basic physiology and, to a lesser extent, sex and squealing.

The basic bodily functions of an inmate receive a high level of attention in a cell. In modern societies, activities like farting, burping, sneezing, spitting, defecating, urinating, or masturbating are commonly associated with strong norms. An unfortunate person in need of relief usually tries to carefully hide the relevant activity from his peers' eyes. Passing an accidental and loud fart in public is universally interpreted as thoroughly embarrassing. Subcultures that relax physiology-related norms tend to be built on close fraternal bonds or a radical contestation of the larger society. In prison, corresponding "dirty physiology" norms simply reflect scarcity of space and air.

Farting, defecation, and urination produce unpleasant externalities for a bystander's nose and ears locked in scarce space. Maintaining ordinary norms would be costly. Recall that the air volume per inmate averages 3–4 m^3 and that the airflow is slow. Since the prison food is of a miserable quality, flatulence is both common and smelly. Smells that form inside a cell persist for a long time. A coherent cluster of prison norms demand that an inmate's intention to fart, defecate, or urinate be made public in advance. Eating while another inmate is engaged in these activities is considered a self-offense. Inmates of all castes are expected to comply with these "dirty physiology norms."

Farting

The intention of passing gas must be loudly announced. The question is asked in a standard format: "Consuming?" After a while, the inmate proceeds with a follow-up announcement: "Do not consume!" Then, he is allowed to relieve himself. His comrades are then free to *add to the pool* with a brief comment "Pool!" Inmates often use the opportunity to add to the pool and a single announcement may initiate a joyful chain reaction across the cell. Amazingly, experienced grypsmen seem to be capable of passing gas continuously for a long period of time or creating a fart at will. The frequency of "consuming" and "do-not-consume" announcements is so high that many suckers call grypsmen "consumers."

Farts differ. A *single* fart may be *silent*, get *internalized*, or even *fail* to materialize. It may easily become a *double* or even a long string of short multiple ones, called *bees* or *bumblebees*. When stinky, a fart is called a *skunk*, or *kiszczak*, after the secret police minister General Kiszczak whose name translates as *gutter*. An unfortunate inmate may produce a wet fart that is accompanied by a *blot*. As the above examples illustrate, the principal dimensions in the prison classification of farts include the number of iterations, loudness, smell, and wetness.

When dealing with bowel movements it is good to be open about it and have a sense of humor. There is no problem if an accidental kiszczak happens. One may save his dignity even when dealing with blots. However, if an inmate tends to consistently produce kiszczaks over a long or short period of time, his peers expect that he will deal with the problem properly. A polite solution is to stick one's bottom to the gate's valve or to the window in order to blow as much bad air outside the cell as possible.

An interesting and universal pattern of behavior is displayed by rookies. A rookie who listens for the first time to farting announcements and multiple detonations is amused, confused, terrified, and, most of all, embarrassed and disgusted. His peers quickly tell him the rules and that he is expected to abide by them. He readily agrees but he does not take the message seriously. In fact, he prepares himself mentally to go *undercover*.

Let's analyze formally the decision problem facing a rookie or any inmate feeling that his bowels are bloated. Various versions of this problem may arise when the compliance with some norm is expected. The specifics of every dilemma depend obviously on the availability of monitoring methods and relevant physical constraints. In all cases, an inmate must decide whether to comply with the norm or to break it. At first, actual calculation of some sort may be involved, not necessarily involving precise estimates of all

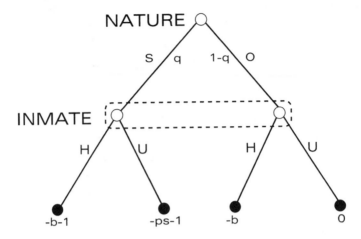

Figure 4.1. The farting dilemma.
Note: S—skunk; O—odorless; H—herald; U—go undercover. The "bad smell" factor is normalized at −1; the "shame" factor is equal to $b > 0$; the sanction is $s > 0$; and the probability of identifying an undercover inmate, given that a skunk happened, is $p > 0$.

relevant probabilities and parameters. However, once an optimal strategy is figured out, it becomes a habit.

In the Farting Dilemma, we assume for simplicity that an inmate can make his fart silent at will. However, he does not know in advance whether it will be a skunk (he estimates the probability of such an event as q) or odorless (subjective probability is $1 - q$). The inmate may comply with the norm and herald his intention loudly or break the norm and go undercover. We assume that his payoff is assembled additively from three components. First, the announcement makes him embarrassed and reduces his utility by b. When the fart is a skunk, he suffers a cost of 1 due to the bad smell. Finally, when he goes undercover and is singled out by his peers as the norm violator, he is punished by a sanction s. He estimates the conditional probability of such an event given that the fart is a skunk as p (see figure 4.1).

Simple arithmetic shows that the announcement makes the inmate better off than going undercover if and only if $b < qps$. Thus, an inmate that announces his intention to fart must consider the embarrassment to be relatively small compared to the expected sanction for breaking the norm and the probability of producing an undercover skunk. While this finding is rather trivial, it is interesting to see how the numbers are actually estimated by various kinds of players.

A rookie enters prison with his subjective estimates that formed while he was at large. The embarrassment factor b is big, the probability of a skunk is low, and the probability that an undercover skunk will be detected is virtually zero. Under the circumstances, he also estimates the sanction s as small. Thus, the expected sanction qps is smaller than the embarrassment for a typical rookie. No wonder that almost every rookie initially goes undercover.

And this is his mistake. The old inmates estimates' are different and more accurately take into account prison constraints. First, the embarrassment factor for an old inmate is almost null. Second, he knows that the probability of passing a skunk when eating prison food is substantial. Third, the sanctions for going undercover are underestimated by the rookie. For old inmates, they are significant. For a new inmate, the sanctions are quite sizeable at the beginning and grow over time when his noncompliance is substantiated. Finally, an old inmate estimates that noncompliance can be detected pretty easily because of the tight space and his cellmates' shrewdness. Thus, an old inmate estimates that $b < qps$. Under these circumstances, heralding is a dominant strategy.

Not only does an old inmate have a different estimate of his own payoffs, but he intuitively understands the model's implications. He may not calculate the odds but he is acutely aware of the dilemmas facing both the rookie and the other old inmates. He can deduce that only the rookie has an incentive to go undercover, while the old inmates herald. When an undercover skunk happens, there is only one category of inmates who could pass it: the rookies. A rookie who never farts or adds to the pool is a particularly likely suspect.

Thus, when a skunk happens, the surprised rookie is immediately blamed. There is no presumption of innocence in prison and he is immediately sanctioned for his violation. At first, he may get a forehead blow and a verbal reprimand. When he stubbornly refuses to cooperate, the sanctions get tougher. His *America* may get longer or he may even be forbidden to join the grypsmen. When he decides to cooperate, he quickly reduces his personal embarrassment factor to zero. I was often under the impression that the old inmates truly enjoy initiating the action and adding to the pool. Incidentally, the English word "fart" signifies "happiness" in argot.

Defecation and Urination

As the reader will recall, the toilet bowl is called *jaruzel* after the chairman of Polish communist party General Jaruzelski. Defecation or urination in prison is called *feeding the jaruzel*. An intention to feed the jaruzel must be heralded as loudly and clearly as farting. Cell inmates learn that the *jaruzel gets lunch* or that *chocolate ice cream is served*. However, while flatulence is essentially not rationed, inmates make a greater effort to coordinate feeding the jaruzel. Frivolous defecation or urination is strictly prohibited. If an inmate announces the intention to defecate or urinate, it is expected that other inmates stay alert and join him even if they do not particularly need to do so.

If necessary, a defecating inmate may receive feedback on his performance. Other inmates shout that *it is burning* or *frying* and encourage him to *mix*, that is, to keep water running continuously or flush it frequently. Taking proper care of water also prevents the jaruzel from *choking* or *refusing to swallow*. Those who defecate frivolously or forget to mix get clear verbal reprimands. If violations are repeated, the harshness of the sanctions increases. In cells with toilet curtains, a burning newspaper or a spoon of jam may suddenly land on the head of an inmate who carelessly violates defecation norms.

In barns, the ratio of inmates per jaruzel is over forty with a *mono* jaruzel and about twenty with a *stereo* jaruzel compared to about less than ten in small cells. Inmates respond to the scarce access to the jaruzel by strengthening coordination. They feed the jaruzel in the morning, at noon, and during afternoon shifts, waiting patiently in line and quickly completing their business. One can also enjoy extra time on the jaruzel by skipping the daily walk, when the cell is almost empty.

Diarrhea is considered a misfortune and the unlucky inmate is not blamed for it or punished. However, inmates watch carefully how he conducts himself under the contingency. It is expected that he gets out of trouble through an adequate diet or fasting as soon as possible. While his condition is tolerated, his carelessness in dealing with the problem is not.

The coordination of defecation and farting affects the eating practices. Inmates drink almost exclusively during meals and after the evening muster at about 6:00 P.M. At barns, irregular eating is strongly discouraged. Maintaining regular eating and drinking patterns helps to coordinate the inmates' physiological cycles. An inmate willing to eat between regular meals is expected to announce his intention loudly: "Attention, consumption!" He may also ask less formally, "Gentlemen, keep your sphincters tight" or "Do not grunt with your rectums." Eating is prohibited when the jaruzel is *hungry* or *thirsty*, that is, when the toilet cover is raised.

When eating and farting collide, the eater feels offended. The farter is more often blamed for the accident. However, the exact verdict depends on who failed to make his intention common knowledge. A rookie who forgets to announce and starts consuming his goodies may be punished with a cautionary fart. Continuing to eat and pretending that nothing happened is an unwise reaction. A better answer is to stop eating, spit the food out, acknowledge the mistake, apologize, and declare no hard feelings toward the punisher. Infrequently, eating may overlap with defecation. Such accidents are usually treated more seriously as they convey strong signals that either the eater or the defecator's alertness is deficient. If there is a clear perpetrator, then he suffers punishment, including relegation to the caste of suckers in extreme cases. If no party is willing to acknowledge the mistake, it may lead to a conflict fueled by pressure on the eater to defend his honor. The lack of any reaction on the part of an offended eater is interpreted as a weakness. Thus, a typical reaction minimally involves strong words and aggressive posturing.

While eating has some priority over dirty physiology during the day, the default rights assignment changes just before going to bed. Around 8:30–9:00 the *curfew* is announced in the cell. Until breakfast, eating is prohibited. The curfew is a happy time when inmates can freely urinate, fart, defecate—and masturbate.

Codes of Squealing, Reporting, and Other Activities

Squealing for police or prison administration is one of the most serious offenses in prison. The norm is public and simple: do not do it under any circumstances. Sanctions for disclosed squealing may include one's relegation to a lower caste. In a serious case they may include a severe beating, rape, or even a death sentence. Only slightly weaker sanctions face an inmate who reports to the prison authorities that he was lightly beaten, forced to do cell chores, or otherwise moderately victimized. Beating rarely comes randomly and it is usually regarded by grypsmen as a legitimate punishment for what is defined as an offense. Staying tough and loyal even under such circumstances may help a sucker to get better treatment or even an upgrade to the grypsmen caste. In general, a grypsman may expect relegation to a lower caste for squealing or reporting, while a sucker or fag may expect a toughening of his treatment and a suspension of some of his meager rights.

Masturbation is closely connected to various secret norms which will be explained in the next section. In most cells, daily masturbation is unwelcome. At a minimum, it must be announced in a similar fashion to "dirty physiology" activities and separated temporally from eating.

Some maxims or rules of thumb referring to various types of frequent interactions are shared by all inmates. "Do not fuck with other inmates' business" recommends neutrality during fights and other conflicts. When talking—rarely—about their sentences and crimes, inmates politely pretend that they believe the presumed innocence of the others. Open questioning or joking at one's declared innocence may be dangerous and induce conflict and hard feelings.

There are also various puzzling empirical regularities related to eating that are easy to detect but difficult to explain within the semi-secret code. Some inmates eat their meals at the table and others eat on their beds or stools. There may be an inmate in the cell who eats sitting on the jaruzel. All such regularities follow the application of a more complex set of norms of the secret code.

THE SECRET CODE

A grypsman learns the essentials of the secret code at the end of his initiation, during the nightly secret training. The training covers general fundamental norms or guidelines (*principles*), the *purity* of cell objects, derived specific norms (*behavioral rules* or *situation rules*), changes in caste membership, the meaning of fag-making, little games or other tests and, finally, argot vocabulary, its grammar and language games. At the time of training a grypsman candidate already speaks some argot and complies with the basic norms. Now, he should master both the letter and the spirit of grypsing. He commits to protecting his knowledge from the curious eyes and ears of nongrypsmen and to passing it on to qualified candidates. If asked by the administration, he has to admit his caste membership openly unless special circumstances arise. He must not attack or offend other grypsmen with no good reason.

Principles are the constitution of grypsing. Actions or activities that violate the spirit of principles are the most serious offenses. An exception to a norm is motivated by a reference to a conflict with some principle. Principles are operationalized through more specific behavior rules.

A handy intellectual shortcut that helps to understand many behavioral rules is the purity classification of cell objects. It constitutes a separate chapter of secret knowledge and provides a large number of exam questions.

Behavioral rules operationalize principles with a catalogue of recommendations for specific situations or objects. There is a lot of variance here: behavioral rules may differ between prisons, cellblocks, and even between cells. They include all semi-secret norms, such as the dirty physiology norms and various rules regulating intercaste interactions.

Caste mobility is the most neglected part of prison university. Usually, various ceremonies of downgrading or upgrading an inmate, or rules of cursing, are covered thoroughly. However, the exact sanctions that are applied are not clearly specified. The interpretation of this set of vague norms is in the hands of the most powerful grypsmen and depends on their interests and the distribution of power.

The last component of prison university—the training of argot vocabulary, argot grammar, and mastering language games—is discussed separately in chapter 5.

The "Pentalogue" of Principles

The *principles* of grypsing are a grypsman's catechism. A grypsman candidate must recite them smoothly and explain their meaning when awakened by an instructor at midnight. The five principles of grypsing are *honor, hygiene, solidarity, noncooperation,* and *help.* The recommendations apply to other grypsmen but not to suckers or fags. Many other norms and argot rules specify further the recommendations of the pentalogue, especially the principle of protecting a grypsman's honor.[1]

Upholding the grypsmen honor code is the most important of all principles, sort of a meta-principle that often overlaps with other rules. A grypsman must defend his honor against three threats from other inmates or personnel: an attack, physical offense, or verbal offense. The precise definition of an offense is provided by various behavioral and argot rules. He is also obliged to avoid untouchable objects, squealing and secretly reporting to the administration. When a grypsman wants to emphasize his words in the strongest possible way, he swears "To my beloved freedom!", "As I love freedom!" or "I will not see freedom anymore if I am lying!" By swearing, he puts his honor at stake.

Observing strict personal hygiene and discipline is supposed to preserve an inmate's sanity, minimize negative externalities on the others, and prevent an epidemic. The public rules of dirty physiology belong partially to this category. A grypsman should cleanse his hands immediately after feeding the jaruzel. He should wash twice a day and brush his teeth with salt if toothpaste is not available. If space permits, he should work out. He should limit or entirely avoid daily masturbation. An exception is *derby*, group onanism practiced by the youngest inmates but disapproved of by older ones. Falling into depression, or silting, is perceived as a lack of mental discipline and is punished.

Solidarity breeds cooperation among grypsmen in their endeavors against the administration. It manifests itself most clearly in maintaining the grypsmen's communication network. Grypsmen pass grypses and various goods around the prison and into the outside world, especially when they work as corridormen. Solidarity forbids stealing from a grypsman and fraud happens quite rarely. However, a grypsman is free to steal from, or cheat, a sucker. Grypsmen help other grypsmen who were attacked by suckers, fags, or members of a different local group. When a grypsman is beaten by guards, other grypsmen should react by relentlessly hitting the gate with stools or table until the guards back off. Grypsmen are also supposed to support prison riots and protests when one is started with good reason. However, since protests happen rarely, and riots are even less frequent, this particular norm refers to a situation that an overwhelming majority of grypsmen will not face. Thus, it is more of an abstract declaration of intentions than a practical guide for action.

Noncooperation with the administration mainly prohibits voluntary cooperation for one's own benefit when other grypsmen may be hurt. The ban on squealing and reporting overlaps with the recommendations of the honor principle. Noncooperation goes further and forbids many forms of fraternization with the personnel, including friendly argot references to less hostile or more permissive guards. Various symbolic forms of cooperation are excluded as well. However, cooperation that benefits both fellow grypsmen in the cell or a larger entity and the administration without hurting other grypsmen is allowed. Moreover, starting unmotivated fights with the administration that may result in the suspension of privileges and the implementation of a stricter regime is discouraged.

While the principle of helping weaker grypsmen seems bogus at first, it becomes more meaningful when one defines weakness appropriately. A weakness of body deserves help, while a weakness of spirit is not tolerated. A case of relaxing the very strong norm of *penis-touching* when super-tough Robin Hood became partially paralyzed is described in the Postscriptum chapter. In general, the norm of help applies to a temporarily needy or sick grypsman rather than a permanently disabled or weak one. Thus, grypsmen on hardbeds, especially powerful elders, regularly get a few cigarettes or small amounts of other goods from volunteering cells. Food is often discreetly smuggled to isolated grypsmen who are on a hunger strike. Virtually all hunger-strikers try to get some food and, simultaneously, to convince the personnel that they are starving.

The Purity of Objects

According to the secret training, all *objects* of the prison world are divided into three categories: *pure*, *dirty*, and *untouchable* (or *fagotized*). The food of a grypsman may be in contact only with pure objects. Such objects can also be touched by hand. Examples of objects that are pure under normal circumstances include a grypsman's own or other grypsmen's cleaned plates, mugs and spoons, dish-towels, the table top, the interior of Titanic, and the scoop.

Dirty objects can be touched with some body parts but cannot come into contact with food. Examples of dirty objects include bunks, stools, blankets and other bedding, most personal belongings, clothes, the sink, floor, walls, gate, window, tigerbars, and an inmate's own penis and anus.

No body part can touch an untouchable object. Examples of untouchable objects include the interior of the jaruzel, the lower part of the *scepter* (toilet brush), the bottom part of the *crown* (toilet cover), the small square of metal floor around the jaruzel, the rag used to clean the toilet, excrement, and the penis of another man.

Conscious and uncoerced physical contact with an object of lower purity may degrade, or *fagotize*, an object or a person. The ubiquitous word "fagotization" may denote that an object has broken, a step-down in an object or person's status to a lower category, or its relegation to the lowest status or caste. Thus, a rookie who fails the fag-making test and agrees to sexually please a grypsman becomes a fag as a consequence of his uncoerced and conscious touching of a grypsman's penis. The emphasis on "uncoerced and conscious" constrains to a large extent the grypsmen's actions in the fag-making test and reduces rapes. However, the condition of "uncoerced and conscious contact" is not necessary for fagotization. A physical contact, even when it is unclear whether it was "uncoerced" or "conscious," may still lead to fagotization if the cell elders so decide. The norm is underspecified and what happens depends on the situational context and local power relations. The rationale grypsmen provided for being so harsh often points out the incentive effects. Being tough on the "uncoerced" and "conscious" parts creates incentives on the part of grypsmen for a sterner effort to avoid trouble and to seek relevant information. When coerced or unconscious fagotization occurs, a grypsman's honor is saved when he sends an exculpating signal to his peers and commits a self-injury.

Precise transition rules that regulate changes in the object's status through touching or coming into physical contact with another object are complex and idiosyncratic. In general, pure objects must be handled especially carefully when in contact with dirty objects and under no circumstances can they come into contact with untouchable objects. Even dirty objects should be handled with care in the vicinity of untouchable objects. Touching an untouchable object is extremely likely to result in fagotization. An object may also get fagotized even with no physical contact. Recall that if one is eating, his food gets fagotized when the jaruzel is hungry, or when somebody else farts. Thus, the entire set of dirty physiology rules that are publicly known receives a more general justification in the secret code.

In some cases, dirty and untouchable objects can be purified. A hand of a grypsman can be purified simply by cleansing it. Various idiosyncratic rules of purification may be introduced in need, when a great number of grypsmen was fagotized by coercion or important cell objects were fagotized maliciously. However, most untouchable objects keep their status permanently.

This purity classification mirrors the three-caste division of inmates. Objects that are related to or belong to a lower-caste inmate move down the hierarchy or at most preserve their purity status. Under radical interpretation, almost all body parts and all possessions of a fag are untouchable. Exceptions include those parts that must be touched during intercourse. Thus, many grypsmen follow the safe strategy of keeping away from a fag—or rather forcing a fag to keep away from them. Paradoxically, this makes a fag's belongings safer from stealing than those of a sucker.

During the secret training, only basic cell objects existing under normal circumstances are explicitly allocated to the three categories. A grypsman must be able to infer the purity status of other objects from the status of related objects, various norms, and common sense. The final exam puts great weight on both the letter and spirit of purity classification and includes a multiple-choice section. A grypsman candidate may be asked a classic tricky question: "What kind of object is a fag's asshole?" Surprisingly, the correct answer is that it is a dirty object. The reasoning is as follows. It is not pure since even one's own anus is not pure. Since a grypsman is allowed to penetrate it with his penis, it can be touched. Thus, it is not untouchable. It is the fag's penis that is untouchable.

The purity classification is presented during the secret training as the exhaustive and disjoint division of all objects into subsets. It makes an attempt to provide a simple explanation for many specific norms and to justify instances of degradation. However, it quickly fails when "exceptions," "corrections," and "problems" become apparent. If a grypsman made a list of all the typical cell "objects" at any specific moment and had accurate information about his world, he could probably extend the purity classification to all objects in an unambiguous fashion. When questions of time, incomplete information, or distinctions among body parts become relevant, problems abound. In fact, both the purity status of various objects and many transition rules describing status changes are incompletely defined.

Thus, an attempt to reconstruct a more precise purity classification than the simplistic version provided at the secret training must take into account additional variables. The purity status of objects may vary over inmates, body parts, and time. An inmate's penis is a dirty object for the owner but it is an untouchable object for a nonowner. The fact that a dirty object may be touched with some body part does not imply that it can be touched with a different part. Again, a canonical example is a fag's asshole that cannot be touched with a grypsman's hand. Moreover, the purity status of certain objects periodically changes over time. A trivial example is a plate that may become temporarily dirty and then regain its purity. However, the changes may be more comprehensive. The hand of grypsman X may be a pure object (immediately after cleansing), dirty (the default status), or untouchable (immediately after feeding the jaruzel) for grypsman Y. Finally, another problem is introduced by incomplete information. For instance, a sucker may pretend to be a grypsman and consequently misrepresent the purity status of his hand or plates.

There is even more ambiguity with transition rules. Many norms are strongly context-dependent and subject to interpretation by the elders. Under special circumstances, the elders can also suspend or relax certain norms. Bending the norms according to one's interests is where the inequities within the grypsmen group manifest themselves most strongly. Moreover, in addition to a "regular" change of status, an object such as the floor may be cursed by a fellow grypsman and become temporarily untouchable under some circumstances. A sucker may forcefully put a grypsman in contact with an untouchable object. While the threat of such an attack may be somewhat limited by smart prevention, every grypsman is vulnerable regardless of his virtues. Such an attack may either lead to the fagotization of a grypsman or it may force him into committing self-injury.

The pervasiveness of logical problems obscures the applicability of universal statements. Even if no uncertainty about an object's status is involved, just fixing the basic logical inconsistencies in the classification of objects without resorting to exceptions requires a relation with at least four variables: An object x is {pure, dirty, untouchable} for grypsman Y's body part w under circumstances z. This complexity feeds the growth of specific and narrowly defined rules. The sources of problems—incomplete definitions of the degree of purity and the transition rules—are not explicitly recognized in the secret training. However, the consequences of problems are clearly present in numerous case studies. No wonder that the attempts at clarification and simplification result in a great number of idiosyncratic behavior rules. This puts slow-witted inmates at a disadvantage and puts a premium on intuition as well as calculation.

Behavioral Rules

Behavioral rules permit, recommend, or require certain courses of action. The purity classification is more or less explicitly embedded in the rules. In some cases, the relevant power of the sucker group is taken into account and a relaxation of the norms is permitted. The rules are formulated as imperatives: in situation x, or with respect to object w, and under conditions y, it is {prohibited, permitted, recommended, required} that you do v. It is possible to shorten this list of imperatives since a requirement to take an action from set A is equivalent to being prohibited from taking an action from $\bar{A}$ (the complement of A). However, the norms listed below preserve the original form. Some have a brief comment or indication of the relative strength of the norm.

Certain behavioral rules formulate recommendations that I described earlier; such rules are omitted. Rules dealing with multiple situations or objects overlap. For instance, a behavioral rule that forbids eating with a sucker at the same table appears in the training period three times—when rules referring to "eating," "sucker," and "table" are discussed. Below, repetitions, obvious rules related to purity classification, or less important rules are omitted. Thus, only a small subset of all rules discussed during the secret training is listed.

FOOD

Prohibited: being in direct contact with dirty and untouchable objects; sometimes prohibited: being handled by a sucker corridorman.

EATING

Prohibited: in the walkspaces, in the corridor (because of the danger of an accidental fart), when the jaruzel is hungry, during the curfew.

Required: observing dirty physiology norms (see the detailed description earlier in this chapter).

HAND OF ANOTHER INMATE

Prohibited: hand-shaking with suckers, fags, personnel, and various categories of external visitors. Exceptions: brother, father, a grypsman's lawyer, and a physician who saved a grypsman's life. Especially dangerous: fag's hand.

Permitted: hand-shaking with other grypsmen. Exceptions: immediately after feeding the jaruzel or in the morning before washing hands.

Required: asking an unknown inmate if he is a grypsman before accepting a hand-shake.

ONE'S OWN HAND

Required: immediate cleansing of one's hand after touching one's own penis or defecating.

PENIS OF ANOTHER INMATE

Prohibited: touching it or being touched by it. The most dangerous object in the cell!

JARUZEL'S NEIGHBORHOOD

Prohibited: walking bare foot, leaving socks up to dry.

BATH

Required: staying sufficiently far away from other inmates; if it is crowded, covering one's penis with a hand to protect other grypsmen and to prevent retaliation from a grypsman who is accidentally fagotized with one's penis.

WALK

Recommended: staying in the cell with a sucker or fag when he skips the walk to control his activity and make squealing more difficult, robbing a sucker when he goes for a walk.

VISITING REHAB OR DOCTOR

Expected behavior: avoiding contact except for an important reason.

Prohibited: signing a sheet of paper in blanco at a rehab's office, a frequent trick applied by administration. The signed paper may then be used during interrogations or to trick other inmates into believing that the signature-holder cooperated with the administration.

Recommended: signing up for a visit when a local sucker or fag signs up, to control his activity.

ENTERING A SUCKER CELL

Required: hitting the gate and demanding a transfer to a grypsing cell.

Recommended: Committing a light self-injury (cutting veins) when there are obstacles preventing a transfer.

ROOKIE

Permitted: fagotizing a rookie if he voluntarily agrees to sexually please another inmate.

SUCKER

Prohibited: eating at the table with grypsmen, touching grypsmen's plates, keeping his plates jointly with grypsmen's plates, fraternizing with grypsmen, letting him sleep in a bunk over a grypsman's bunk, letting him sleep in a bunk when a grypsman sleeps on the floor mattress.

If eating at the same table is unavoidable, the table should be covered with a blanket.

Recommended: forcing him to clean the cell, handle the cube and laundry.

Required: keeping him unaware of the cell's secret transaction and communication channels.

Permitted: robbing and cheating him.

FAG

Almost all rules applicable to sucker apply to fag. Exception: fag's belongings may be untouchable and should not be stolen.

Required: forcing a fag to clean the jaruzel and its neighborhood, stay around the jaruzel, eat on the jaruzel's cover, giving him a feminine name and referring to him as "she."

Permitted: forcing him into intercourse, preferably oral, with a grypsman assuming the active role.

CELL KEYS

Prohibited: keeping them, picking them up from the floor, or handing them to a guard; in the most radical version: touching them. The justification of this rule refers to the symbolic meaning of the cell's key as a tool of enslavement.

CELL LIGHTBULB

Prohibited: short-circuiting the lightbulb for fun.

ACCIDENTAL OR MALICIOUS FAGOTIZATION BY SUCKERS OR PERSONNEL

Recommended: Avoiding dangerous places and concentrations of suckers (in prison).

Required (when facing a clear and present danger): Crying for other grypsmen's help.

Expected behavior after accidental or malicious fagotization: committing light self-injury (cutting veins).

Familiarity with behavioral rules and purity classification are often tested jointly. A particular object or situation is mentioned and a candidate must recite all related behavioral rules or withstand cross-examination:[2]

HAND

Q: Who can you shake hands with?

A: Other grypsmen, father, brother, lawyer, doctor who saved my life.

Q: When is a grypsman's hand untouchable?

A: After he feeds the jaruzel and in the morning before he cleanses it.

Q: An unknown inmate offers you a hand-shake. What will you do?

A: Ask if he is a grypsman.

Q: What kind of object is a fag's hand?

A: Untouchable.

Q: Can you shake it after you fuck the fag to show your gratitude?

A: No.

Q: What should you do after waking up?

A: Immediately wash my hands.

Q: Why?

A: Because my hand could touch my penis during the night and I could fagotize another grypsman with a hand-shake.

Q: You didn't masturbate last night. Should you still wash your hand?

A: Yes. I could touch my penis unconsciously while sleeping.

A standard pair of yes-no questions that combine purity and behavior knowledge is closely related to the problem associated with the purity of a fag's ass. The first question is: "Is a grypsman allowed to shit on a fag's penis?" and a follow-up question reverses the roles. Rookies typically answer "yes" and "no" to these questions, respectively. The correct answers are just opposite. A grypsman is "not allowed to shit on a fag's penis" since he could accidentally touch the fag's penis and get fagotized. The reader may recall the fact that a fag's bottom is a dirty object, not an untouchable one, and figure out the rationale behind the second answer.

SANCTIONS AND INTERCASTE MOBILITY

All grypsmen enforce their code to some extent. Enforcers enjoy respect from the others. In cases of doubt or serious violations, the norms are interpreted by the elders, the local grypsmen elite, or by a local *fuss-master*, the grypsmen leader. There are hierarchies among the elders and fuss-masters in the cell, cellblock, and prison levels. A grypsman is supposed to know the elder or fuss-master at the level immediately above his own, all grypsmen at his own cell or cellblock level, and all grypsmen under his own direct jurisdiction. However, the identity of major grypsmen leaders quickly becomes common knowledge, available both to well-informed suckers and the personnel. The elders initiate the character tests applied to rookies, impose their interpretation of the tests' results, prescribe sanctions for offenses, and suspend or modify norms. The power of norm-interpretation and conflict-arbitration translates into lucrative profits. It is somewhat constrained both by the strong norms of intragrypsmen brotherhood and the fierce competition for power. A self-appointed arrogant dictator could easily be turned into a sucker when a powerful group of his subordinates decide to take the risk of *spinning an affair* against him.

The fuss-master's life is busy and tiresome.

The presence of a [major] grypsmen leader in a cell creates a constant tension. He engages in neverending window conversations, adjudicates conflicts among grypsmen, threatens, curses, and forgives.[3] Searches, rehab visits, and reports are more frequent and constitute an extra hassle for the other inmates, who happen to be in such a cell. Somebody is always passing grypses, knocking on the wall, and shouting from a walk-place. A fuss-master often has adjutants, typically youngsters. Adjutants handle grypses and answer window calls on the fuss-master's behalf. They frequently get reports and go to hardbed. But they also catch scraps of splendor and glory, they witness great things, and contribute to history-making.[4]

When a particularly strong norm is violated, there is little dis-cretion in sanctioning. This happens when an inmate agrees to provide sexual favors or is deciphered as a squealer. Weaker viola-tions result in forehead blows, *carrots* (wet-towel blows), and verbal punishments. The accumulation of minor offenses indicating low alertness, weak intellect, or an unwillingness to conform, may result in a major sanction. In less serious or doubtful cases, sanctions de-pend strongly on the context and the idiosyncratic interpretation of the elders.

Sanctions for verbal offenses or minor violations are applied on the spot. For serious violations, a major sanction may immediately follow in a clear case or it may be applied after some time when the corresponding *affair* is fully substantiated. *Spinning an affair* denotes a grypsman's attempt to gather evidence, impose an inter-pretation, and collect sufficient support for defining an event as a serious violation of norms that potentially deserves a major sanc-tion. The goal of a larger affair is usually to confirm that some gryps-man is a squealer, ensign, or that he is testifying in an ongoing investigation and is *selling* his colleagues out. A less serious affair may unfold as follows:[5]

Tiger from cell 15 gives Barber five packets of tea and asks him for same-day delivery to Donald Duck from 35 at a fee of one packet. In the evening Donald Duck signals that he got only three packets. Tiger spins an affair and contacts Barber. The latter explains that the last cell he shaved today was 30. He took his one packet and asked the corridorman Zorro to deliver the rest during the dinner. Donald Duck from 35 con-firms that he got the stuff from Zorro. Zorro confirms that he took a packet for himself as a customary risk fee. At this point, Tiger has all of the relevant information and decides that the affair is clearly a minor one. Now the bargaining takes place among Tiger, Donald Duck, Zorro, and Barber about whether Barber and Zorro were entitled to a packet each, whether they should split it, or whether one of them should keep everything.

Two ultimate sanctions include the relegation of a rookie or grypsman to sucker status or the fagotization of a grypsman or a sucker.

Degradation follows a failure in little games or baptism. It can also occur when an inmate commits a pretty serious offense, such as reporting some cell activity to the administration, or when he squeals. If Barber were found guilty of stealing one packet, his offense could also lead to degradation. The offended grypsman or a grypsman who represents the local community then curses the degraded inmate ceremonially with a strong blaspheme: "Go to sack, you fucking sucker!", "Fuck yourself!", "Dick in your ass, you fucking sucker!" Alternatively, he simply calls him a dirty dick, pussy, pussy-licker, etc. The symbolic cursing is accompanied by a couple of strong fist or forehead blows.

"Failure" in tests is often subject to interpretation. In one instance of a barn's baptism, four candidates were waiting in line. When two inmates failed and were degraded, Student, the next in line, refused to take the test to make a statement of solidarity with the two rookies. The test was suspended and the three local elders held an emergency meeting. In an unusual scenario, an elder was delegated to carry a gryps to Student: "The test is fake, nobody will be beaten." While Student answered that he knew this fact and still refused, the meeting re-assembled and reached a surprising verdict. Student, it was decided, was admitted to the test by mistake. He was in fact too experienced an inmate to be subject to such test and he refused justly. He was exempted. The last rookie waiting in line benefitted since the fake character of the test became apparent at that time and he passed the test by default.

It turned out that this surprising verdict was reached because Student was apparently too valuable a personal companion for the elders to be degraded. He had taught the elder who carried to him the message how to play bridge. This activity could have been terminated if Student had become a sucker. Even more important was the support of a silent nonelder grypsman, treated with ceremonial reverence by all elders, who supposedly was the chief Rakowiecka fuss-master. It turned out that the powerful grypsman suffered from a pancreas malfunction similar to that of Student. When Student entered the barn, he was granted an interview with the presumed fuss-master general. When he learned about the fuss-master's problems, he offered advice and shared his medications. Since then, they often talked about their health problems, faking illness, and self-injuries. The fuss-master found Student's expertise valuable. At some point, he uncovered to Student his plans of self-injury and followed Student's advice to maximize his chances of contracting a hepatitis A or B virus. Clearly, the degradation of a useful advisor who was generally harmless was at odds with the fuss-master's interests.[6]

Degradation is personalized. Unless a sucker did not want to join grypsmen at entry, he was degraded by a particular *curse-holder*, the grypsman who cursed him. If Barber were found guilty of stealing tea, Tiger could curse him and become his curse-holder. Having a stable of cursed suckers is potentially profitable. Profits are hidden in the possibility of reversing a sucker's degradation, that is, upgrading him through a complex and not too frequent ceremony of *lift* or *resurrection*. A consequence of the high profitability of lifting curses is that elders have incentives to over-degrade and look for fake offenses when the proportion of suckers is small enough. Since the risk of administrative punishment for organizing a relatively nonviolent degradation is pretty small, the elders often informally compete for access to difficult and relatively safe tests that may generate a sucker.

The necessary conditions for lifting are the withdrawal of the curse by its holder and a satisfactory demonstration of the sucker's extraordinary toughness. The evidence of toughness must be compelling. Self-injury, fagotization of another inmate, hunger strike, and one's refusal to work are acceptable proofs. Then, if a sucker did not commit a serious offense, withdrawing a curse is negotiable and usually can be bought with a decent ransom paid in cigarettes, tea, or zlotys. When an upgrade is being debated, the particularistic interests of a curse-holder interplay with the objective expectations of a reasonable display of toughness.

In rare cases, elders may become so impressed with a sucker's toughness that they may spontaneously initiate a lift. In my barn, a sucker volunteered to work with grypsmen all night on a major project. A grypsman inadvertently crushed the sucker's finger with a hammer-like device. The heavily bleeding sucker bravely withstood the pain and decided not to sign up for a doctor's visit. Upon learning about the incident, the cell elders called a meeting, recommended that the sucker visit a doctor, and started a rehabilitation procedure. Grypses were sent to the curse-holder and possible witnesses. Unfortunately, I was released from prison before the case was concluded.[7]

Once all of the evidence is collected, all curses are withdrawn, and the support of the elders or fuss-masters is secured or bought, the lifting ceremony takes place. A curse-holder makes a laudatory speech or, if he is in a different cell, a designated grypsman loudly reads his conciliatory statement secretly smuggled from another cell or cell-block. Next, all cell grypsmen solemnly shake the former sucker's hand. However, lifting does not erase the stigma completely. When a grypsman-turned-sucker-turned-grypsman commits another offense and becomes a sucker again, a prison maxim says that a second lift does not happen. In fact, I never heard about a second lift.

Fagotization, a less frequent but more dramatic sanction, follows the most serious offenses. The grypsing code leaves little discretion here. An inmate becomes a fag after a failed fag-making test or infrequently, after a rape. When the offense was heavy squealing, fagotization is usually conducted with the help of an untouchable object. The victim's head or hand is put into the jaruzel and the water is flushed. He may be sprinkled with a scepter or pissed on. His face may be wiped with the toilet rag. He may be forced to brush his teeth with a toothbrush covered with excrement. The latter variant was widely discussed by Białołęka grypsmen in 1985 as a good alternative to more traditional methods. It was considered safer for the punishing grypsmen since it involved little violence that could lead to a sentence. A fagotized inmate may also be *paid a parole:* a grypsman may hit his face with a penis. Sexual versus squealing-related fagotization happens in jail relatively more often than in prison. Inmates vulnerable to fag-making and sexual exploitation usually attain their status early in jail and come to prison with the stigma. Squealing usually follows a comprehensive socialization to the prison environment and is more frequent in prison than in jail.

All cell grypsmen are expected to participate in fagotization. Sometimes local suckers may be invited to join the punishing squad as well and be rewarded for their cooperation. Collective execution disperses responsibility for an action that is more risky than degradation. Moreover, incentives to personalize fagotization are absent since the fag's stigma is irreversible.

A bothersome problem for the grypsmen code is the possibility of malicious fagotization by a sucker or fag. An unsuspecting grypsman may be attacked with a toilet cover, rag, or scepter. A sucker may throw excrement at the fan in the baths or a madman may start pissing at grypsmen. A freshly degraded grypsman may desperately start a *domino* attack on the entire cell with his own penis in order to equalize everybody's status by degradation. While there is an honorable way out of the trouble—a self-injury through vein-cutting—it resembles the rescue option of a disgraced samurai in the eyes of many grypsmen.

Discretional degradation makes secret norms somewhat fuzzy and makes a grypsman's fortune insecure. Everybody can be hit, nobody is immune to a sudden attack or a spun affair. The verdict—"degradation" or "it was not his fault"—may be in the hands of the others. Some grypsmen try to ensure their safety by making their intention to retaliate with a domino public knowledge: "If I were ever degraded, I would degrade everybody else around me." Such threats do not induce sympathy though. Prison rules of thumb say that the best defense against degradation or fagotization is to carefully build one's reputation, form alliances, make no foes, and make oneself useful for everybody.

CHAPTER FIVE

Argot

ARGOT VOCABULARY

Argot, like the prison code of behavior, consists of layers character-ized by varying degrees of secrecy.[1] Complex vocabulary, the first layer, supplies alternative names for all objects, situations, and activ-ities of prison life. Body parts, cell furniture and prison compo-nents, typical activities and situations, psychological states of mind, personnel roles, even many objects of freedom life have their own names. Experienced inmates from all castes use such vocabulary fluently and can smoothly switch between regular names and their argot counterparts. Lower prison personnel are familiar with select words and often use them when communicating with inmates. The degree of familiarity with the argot vocabulary is a function of a person's social role, intelligence, prison tenure, and other variables.

A strong command of argot, imagination in naming, and conver-sational wit are highly valued in prison. Inmates relentlessly attempt to enrich the argot with witty terms and rules. The word *kiszczak* (gutter), denoting a stinky fart with the name of the secret police chief, and based on a word game, is widely considered an argot masterpiece. But what stimulates the inmates' linguistic activity is deeper than the sheer joy of joke-telling. A harsh environment and an overwhelming sense of deprivation reward the art of recreating images of ordinary life, of what is now perceived to be a lost paradise. Assigning to the surrounding objects and prison-specific situations new names provides an illusion of control that somehow heals anxiety. Finally, argot names, rules, and nicknames help to preserve secrecy in various spheres of communication and differentiate grypsmen from other groups.

If a casual spectator interested in inmate argot were allowed to place a webcam in a cell and listen, he could arrive at his first empirical generalization quickly. He would notice that the common physiological and sexual linguistic taboos are nonexistent. The body with its daily physiological and sexual routines is the centerfold of inmates' attention. In their small talk, they refer to their physiological and sexual activities without excitement. Analyses of sexual performance or nonperformance make everyday friendly conversations and feed social interactions. There are about twenty-five different names for penis and most of them are in everyday use. There are slightly fewer names for vagina.

Brutal honesty, like evening tales from the freedom paradise, helps an inmate to maintain a mental distance from his here-and-now. Those unable to adopt the no-compromise open talk on manly affairs do poorly in prison. They are relentlessly mocked, humiliated, or beaten. Their awkward presence reminds grypsmen that they are powerless and that their apparent control of their lives is an illusion. Learning argot vocabulary is the first step toward cutting ties with freedom.

A second observation could be that argot is, to a large extent, a complete language, capable of describing the world from the prison perspective, using its own vocabulary while borrowing syntax and inflection rules from the source language. In argot, a magnifying glass is applied to all the components of the prison world, while various freedom objects not important for prison life are nonexistent. Argot provides very concise and efficient descriptions. I translated into actual argot a number of stories from prison research questionnaires using survey-speak that intended to imitate argot.

The length of an average questionnaire story was shortened by more than half when translated into argot.

On the other hand, if the video function of our webcam researcher were down and he could only listen, he would frequently be unable to attach any meaning to various conversations. Learning vocabulary would be of little help since argot relies strongly on the context. The physical surroundings of the speaker, who refers to an object and utters its name, are often necessary for a sensible interpretation. Various inflections of words such as "bitch," "son-of-a-bitch," "fuck," "fucking," "whore," and, to a lesser extent, "cock," "ass," "pussy," "balls," and "shit" are the principal components of communication. Combinations of these words used within a specific context carry a great variety of meanings.

Consider the following sentence expressing the feelings that a juvenile grypsman decided to share with me: *Whore-your-mum, this fucking bitch fucks with me like a son-of-a-bitch.*[2] This sentence was perfectly understandable only in the context in which it was formulated and had nothing to do with the interlocutor's mother. It was meant to express my friend's deep frustration with the erratic flow of water in the lavatory. Outside of this specific context, the sentence's meaning immediately blurs and it could be used to denote a variety of situations usually regarded as dissimilar.

A part of the semi-secret argot are nicknames. Most inmates bring one with them from freedom or get one at their first entry. Grypsmen and usually sucker's nicknames are restricted by the secret argot rules to nonoffensive ones, while a fag is by default assigned a feminine name. Nicknames are public knowledge in the cell, but grypsmen try to protect them from the personnel. Secrecy helps to preserve the identity of those sending grypses or shouting messages to their pals from a different cell ("Devil listen, Dragon is speaking at the window"). A typical nickname of a career criminal is unrelated to an inmate's publicly known characteristics and refers to neutral symbols, objects, animals, nationalities, and so on, such as Chinese, Frenchmen, Spaniard, Gypsy, Melon, Tarzan, Devil, Tiger, Reagan, Dragon, Herring, Wolf, Gorilla, Prince, Hidalgo. Hitler, barely admissible because of his hatred of communism, was popular among lower strata of grypsmen. Since the communists were held in even lower esteem than the Nazi, such nicknames as Stalin or Lenin were explicitly forbidden by the argot rules and considered offensive. Most *reptiles* (guards) are given their own, usually quite friendly, nicknames. Reptiles often learn their nicknames after some time and offensive ones would make them more aggressive toward inmates.

In sum, the main features of the semi-secret argot include an alternative vocabulary, a strong focus on prison phenomena—especially bodily functions and sex—and high context-dependence. The assignment of nicknames to inmates and lower personnel is protected by the inmates but at least partially decoded by personnel. All these features are quite easily observable and are shared to a large extent by inmates of all castes and lower personnel.

Argot Roles

Sykes painted a fascinating gallery of numerous prison social roles.[3] He argued that labeling and endowing the roles with stereotypes are the critical functions of the inmate argot. By characterizing the types of behavior along the crucial dimensions of "pains of imprisonment"—prison-specific types of deprivation—the inmates provide themselves "with a sort of shorthand which compresses the variegated range of experience into a manageable framework." While the names and importance of these *argot roles* may vary from prison to prison, they seem to be at the center of American prison subculture.[4] The roles "are allocated on the basis of inmates informally observing and assessing the behaviors and verbalizations of a given inmate to a variety of real and contrived situations."[5] The roles are not rigid. Inmates "may play one role in the industrial shops ... and another role in the Wing. A prisoner may quickly assume one role on first entering the institution and then shift to another role at a later point in time."[6]

In Polish prisons, the allocation of main social roles among inmates is ritualized and the resulting labels of grypsman, sucker, and fag are difficult or even impossible to change. The caste membership of an inmate is the main informational shorthand for his peers. Other features are of secondary importance. Nevertheless, observation-based stereotyping exists. Stereotypes are formed similarly as in the American argot, that is, they are motivated by sexual and material deprivation, and the attitude toward other prisoners and the administration. The names are part of the semi-secret argot. Major argot roles in Polish prisons are usually restricted to a subset of inmates from one caste. Most of them refer to suckers, fags, and inmates of uncertain or transitory status. A few names are reserved for the grypsmen elite and other names denote types of unorthodox capabilities. To distinguish between American and Polish argot roles in this section, while both are italicized, the former are set in bold type as well.

Among the lowest roles in American prisons, *fags* are inmates who are inclined toward passive homosexual activity while *punks* are either coerced, or treat it as a means to acquire scarce goods or protection. Equivalents of both types belong to the caste of fags in Polish prison, along with those who violated other serious nonsexual norms and got fagotized without sexual intercourse. The exact way an inmate became a fag is of lesser importance. A sexually active fag is usually treated much better than an inactive one. A squealing fag may expect the harshest treatment.

A *weakling*, a weak and timid inmate, is another lower role in the United States. It is absent in Polish prisons. The equivalents of weaklings become suckers or fags at the initiation stage in Poland. Similarly, the pressure of the grypsmen subculture makes it difficult for a lone Polish prisoner to assume the role of a *center man*, halfway between inmates and administration, that exists in American prisons. Such roles are more likely to emerge when the grypsmen's control over prison life is less firm.

The American role of *squealer* is closest to its Polish counterpart. However, grypsmen assume that all suckers and fags are potential *squealers* anyway and thus isolate them informationally in the cell. A confirmed *squealer* gets a tougher treatment and may be forced to leave the cell. If a sucker squeals, he effectively blocks his chance for a lift to grypsman. Thus, while there is no formal caste of *squeal-*

ers, this particular argot label provides inmates with some valuable information and often serves as a basis for action.

Other lower roles are temporary. Clearly, the most universal is the role of *rookie*, corresponding to the American *fish*. An *aproposman*, who abuses his cellmate's ears with phrases like "apropos" or "excuse me, can I use the bathroom, please," either makes friends with argot or becomes a sucker. A *silter*, who silently laments his lost past or vegetates in depressed stupor, becomes one even faster. A mischievous and feared *ensign* is a former sucker or fag who pretends to be a grypsman in a new location. His role is identified when he gets deciphered. Then, he is severely beaten and fagotized.

There are also a few roles based on an inmate's unorthodox behavioral characteristics. In American prisons, a **tough** is quick to react violently against his cellmates, while a **ball buster** often revolts against the guards. A **hipster** pretends to be tough but his credentials are doubtful. All these types are lumped in Polish prisons into one role, a *jumper*. This mildly disdainful name denotes a grypsman who is not in full control of his emotions and allows them to affect his behavior. A *jumper* is obsessed with code compliance and looks for minor violations in order to spin affairs. He usually fails in his projects and is considered an unreliable partner in complex endeavors. When he makes too much fuss and collides with higher powers in the cell, he becomes good material for demotion to sucker.

A *cat*, an extreme version of *jumper*, is an inmate whose violence and unpredictability verge on insanity. A *cat* is quick to quarrel with other inmates and ready to self-injure himself for fun. *Cats* may be both grypsmen and suckers. In the latter case the unpredictability of their reactions buys them some peace from grypsmen. Especially valuable are formal psychiatric documents that ease the pressure on the *cat* of frequent costly demonstrations of insanity. Thus, suckers or fags often try this avenue of escape from their miserable roles. Two second-degree (light) *cats*-suckers who befriended me confessed that their precious status, backed by documents, resulted from carefully executed plans.[7] The cost was enormous: half a year of posing as a deaf-mute and a long series of self-injuries, respectively. Thus, this avenue is not wide open to everybody. Playing a *cat* requires extreme determination and courage.

The major roles within the top caste denote an inmate's place in the local hierarchy of power. A *fuss-master* is the most influential grypsman at the level of a cell, cellblock, or prison. He is endowed with more or less formal authority to interpret norms, order sanctions, and resolve conflicts. When norm-interpretation is a collegial matter, the member of such a collegium is called an *elder*. The temporary role of a *fuss-maker* denotes an inmate who is presently spinning an affair. Fuss-maker denotes also a more sophisticated version of a *jumper*, a grypsman skillfully using the norms against his peers. A *fuss-maker* is quite familiar with the intricacies of code and uses his expertise at will when he sees benefits. He does not spin affairs randomly, as a *jumper*, but rather goes after carefully selected, easy, and profitable pickings. A villain among villains, often posing as the code and argot zealot, he hunts his victims with cold blood. He may target an innocent rookie who uses "Spearmint" toothpaste and accuse him for auto-fagotization with mint sperm. He may notice a ladybug picture decorating the rookie's soap-box and declare the rookie a covert supporter of an ephemeral caste of *ladybugs*, hostile to grypsmen. Virtually all *fuss-masters* and *elders* have some characteristics of a *fuss-maker*.

The encompassing subculture of grypsmen endows its members with more flexibility and sophistication than that of American inmates. An American *gorilla* bullies weaker inmates in order to extract goods. A *wolf* assumes an active role in a homosexual intercourse. A *merchant* extracts gains from prison trade. A grypsman learns how to play all these and other roles according to circumstances. In fact, he learns many of these skills from his fellow inmates as part of the standard secret training. He bullies a rookie in order to test him and possibly benefit from his misery. He sexually exploits a fag and takes part in prison trade. The capacity for changing roles and performing well in various arenas is highly correlated with a grypsman's status. There is strong pressure to learn new skills and abilities. The vast role-playing expertise desensitizes most experienced grypsmen to bullying and other displays of violence. Such displays are perceived as routine tests that can be easily passed with routine reactions. Above all, in all of his incarnations, a grypsman is supposed to calculate and optimally respond to circumstances, given the constraints of time, place, code, and argot.

SECRET ARGOT GRAMMAR

The prison argot involves more sophistication than a mechanical translation of the freedom language into a set of new names. Its usefulness for the description of the main types of prison behavior is matched by its signaling function. The proper argot grammar is secret and is carefully protected by grypsmen. Some rules leak to outsiders and smart suckers can learn parts of the secret code after years behind bars. However, a nontrained inmate or a personnel member has little chance of learning the entire comprehensive system through observation.

The argot grammar consists of rules that govern the combination of words in addition to, or instead of, the ordinary language grammar. It is mainly constructed around the concept of insulting a grypsman's honor, and is closely connected to principles, rules of behavior, and the purity classification. The argot grammar's special feature is that it divides the set of all freedom cursing phrases into two subsets. The first subset consists of admissible curses. Such curses are welcome, and the fine art of cursing blossoms in prison as nowhere else. The remaining inadmissible curses are called blasphemies. Deliberate or inadvertent blasphemies aimed at a grypsman are serious insults. They may result in a fight and degradation of the insulter or the insulted. Using blasphemies is also forbidden in the neutral context of everyday conversations. Indiscriminate cursing, often applied by naive rookies on entry, signals an unfamiliarity with the secret code and argot rules.

A blasphemy consists of the comparison of a grypsman to a fag, woman, squealer or, though to a lesser degree, prison and enforcement personnel or the communists. Even suggesting such a comparison may be regarded as offensive. The argot grammar operationalizes the concept of an insult through a long list of potentially blasphemous words and specific rules that must be applied to such words. A grypsman must either use a substitute word, or he must "extend" the dangerous word with additional words that neutralize its offensive meaning.

The most insulting blasphemies include a direct declaration such as "I stick my dick in your ass!" or "Fuck you!" They can also involve calling an inmate a (fucking) "fag," "whore," "bitch," "lesbian," "mother-fucker," "cock-sucker," "pussy-eater," "cunt," etc. A ritual and direct blasphemy accompanies degradation and fagotization. Referring to someone directly with a blasphemous phrase is avoided even among close friends in the relaxed atmosphere of a prison hospital.

Indirect blasphemies are more complex and interesting. These blasphemies are apparently neutral words whose applicability is limited by the argot to fag, woman, squealer, penis, prison personnel, communists, and so on. Every case is justified by a relevant explanation of why the particular word is considered offensive. Mastering all of the indirect blasphemies and relevant rules is the most difficult part of learning argot. A small selection of typical indirect blasphemies that often cause accidental offenses is shown in table 5.1. Extending a blasphemous word is supposed to clarify any ambiguity regarding an inmate's intentions. It is allowed only for select indirect blasphemies, and the precise rules for extending them are more complex than is shown in table 5.1. For instance, the verb "pull" is used when a grypsman asks a fag to please him orally. Thus, he cannot ask his fellow grypsman to "pull" when, say, sending a gryps through a digger. "Pull this roll" clarifies the ambiguity. However, "pull this end" is not an acceptable extension. It is even more offensive than "pull" since the "end" is one of many names for penis. Similarly, calling somebody a "pussy" is a serious offense, while a descriptive term "pussy-fed" denotes a pimp.

There is little doubt that the most important phrase in the argot is "kurwa twoja mać." A lexicographic translation of this phrase is "whore (is) your mum." It is omnipresent. One hears it in a cell up to a thousand times a day. The word "whore" is highly blasphemous but, paradoxically, "whore-your-mum" or just "whore-mum" is a properly extended and neutralized expletive. Inmates in different cells offered various explanations for this surprising reversal of

TABLE 5.1.
Major Indirect Blasphemies, Rationale, and Suggested
Substitutes or Neutralizing Extension

Blaspheme	Related to	Substitute or Neutralizing Extension
nice	fag, woman	handsome
give me	prostitute	give me <this object>
beloved	fag, woman	favorite
pull	fag and oral sex	pull <this object>, draw
move	fag and oral or anal sex	shift, move <this object>
push	fag, woman, and anal sex	push <this object>
end	penis	ending
I was lucky	I had intercourse	I was fortunate
luckiness	having intercourse	fortune
small	penis	short, micro
red	communist	scarlet, red <on your face>
after	fag	behind, after <this particular event>
fuck	fag, woman	fuck <it>, fuck <it all>
member	penis, communist	participant
fuck you!	fag	—
whore	woman, fag, personnel	whore-your-mother

Note: Blasphemous words were translated from Polish into their closest English counterparts. Parentheses < > illustrate permissible neutralizing extensions.

meaning. According to one school of thought, "whore-your-mum" originates in the prewar slang of Polish thieves. A thief's family background was often "mother-whore, father-drunk" and admitting such connections was not considered offensive. Another explanation refers to the line one often hears on entry from the warden: "In prison, I am your mother: I feed you, I pamper you, I punish you." A "whore" is one of the more popular names for the members of the prison personnel. A similar rule applies to "son-of-a-bitch" (*skurwysyn*), denoting another widely used and non-blasphemous phrase. "Bitch" on its own is a blasphemy.

There are a handful of idiosyncratic rules and explanations in the grammar of argot. An automatic application of a relevant word may be required in certain contexts. A guard who treats inmates well and ignores minor violations cannot be called a nice, decent, or good man. The required phrase is a *cock-licking reptile* as opposed to a *cock-biting reptile*. The routine explanation is that this is the highest level of humanity a guard can reach. This phrase testifies to the limit of verbal fraternization with the personnel. Whatever the rationale, inmates treat forbidden or required phrases as idioms and follow the rules. Mocking the core argot grammar, unlike its various dialects and peripheral ad hoc rules, is dangerous.

When attacked with a blasphemy, a grypsman may defend his honor by resorting to a physical fight. Cursing back is often not a good strategy since it escalates the fight without removing the stigma. The insulted grypsman alternatively may make up an ad hoc rule that nullifies the insult and try to persuade his watchful audience that this is the right answer. Better yet, like a cornered sorcerer from a fantasy tale throwing the spell of last resort against his enemies, he may call upon the powers of *stepping*, the radical version of argot.

Stepping amplifies the regular argot with even more exclusions and stricter enforcement, and provides more flexible means for fighting against blasphemies and using them strategically. A stepping grypsman may reverse the curse, nullify it, or make it neutral by default if it originates with a nongrypsman.

Stepping may be introduced as a temporary defensive measure, or it may be the norm in a cell, cellblock, or prison. It denotes argot at full throttle, with hypercomplexity and rigorous enforcement. No body part or prison object can be called with its ordinary name. Using such names is forbidden and the blasphemous character of every name is appropriately justified. "Hair" can only refer to pubic hair—grypsmen have "hay" or "feathers"; only women have (vulvar) "lips," and so on (see table 5.2). All names considered blasphemous according to the radical version of argot are present in the standard argot as well, but the associated bans outside stepping are less rigid and vary across cells and prisons.

TABLE 5.2.

Secret Meaning of the Names of Various Body Parts and Functions

Body Part or Function	Secret Meaning
Head	glans
face	vulva, anus
cheek	buttock
mouth	outer vaginal lips
lips	inner vaginal lips
eye	vagina, anus
ear	squealer
hair	pubic hair
nose	penis
Other body parts	
chest	breast
foot	gun
neck, finger	penis
skin	foreskin
Body functions and activities	
drink	urinate
eat	defecate
talk, joke	pass flatulence
ask	penis

Note: Ordinary Polish words were translated into their closest English counterparts. In some cases the secret meaning is based on a word game.

The mainstream argot adopted parts of stepping grammar but did not attach the intended importance to them. Some grypsmen reject stepping entirely or consider its recommendations merely as suggestions for special occasions. Nevertheless, many stepping rules become common knowledge. Various stepping rigors may be introduced temporarily, as a means of rapidly socializing a rookie. And while a typical grypsman likes to mock stepping, he also learns its rules, just in case he gets thrown—temporarily or permanently—into a stepping cell.

In stepping cells life is transformed into a never-ending race and fight. Imagine a testosterone-driven world of predominantly young inmates, a world that regular grypsmen find violent and frightening. Every object may get symbolically cursed or fagotized, de-fagotized, and fagotized for fun. A stepping grypsman can ritually de-fagotize the blasphemy and reverse the curse by using the phrase "back to you." When attacked verbally by a nongrypsman, say, by a warden surrounded by guards, he can think or mutter this phrase instead of speaking it out. Thus, a sucker or guard has no power to offend him. When a fellow grypsman attacks verbally, the response must be loud and it may start an exchange of incantations. Extending the blasphemy by tacking on the phrase "for fun," even after a few weeks or months, nullifies its offensive content. Only the curser himself has the power of nullification. In addition, there are complex and often mutually inconsistent rules of conditional nullification, irreversible blasphemies, or temporary suspensions of various rules.

In a stepping cell, the statement "the weather is nice today" is considered offensive against the weather. As a consequence, the youngsters will skip the walk entirely unless the frivolous or careless curser nullifies his curse. If nullification is locally or temporally suspended, no stepping cell will go out of the building and their wrath may turn against the curse-holder. A youngster's shout "I stick my dick in this doctor!" will be followed by a debate: Can a fagotized physician treat his grypsmen patients? Those who truly need medical attention may refuse to enter the fagotized health-room. Announcing "red water" means that cleansing one's hands implies automatic self-fagotization. Food, clothes, books, cell furniture may get fagotized and, as such, cannot be eaten or touched.

A stream of blasphemies from an angry stepper can contaminate entire cells, cellblocks, worlds. Calling the floor "fagotized" compels his fellow inmates to move to bunks since touching a fagotized floor is prohibited. The statements "dick in the bunks" and "fuck the stools" reduce the allowable space to walls and their equipment. Youngsters must jump on tigerbars, try to climb the gate, sit on a sink, and beg the curser to add "for fun." Then he may cut their cries with the "red air" announcement. Struggling on their last gulp of pure air, watching how impurity takes over their last bastions, steppers may fall onto the untouchable floor, furiously hit the window to escape infamy through self-injury, or attack the curser. There may be no way out of this trap. The blasphemy opens the hell of violence.

Even without the rigors of stepping, observing the ordinary rules of argot is a tough job. A forbidden word or phrase comes to a rookie's tongue amazingly easily. He learns about it from the hardening of the looks around him or, more directly, from a sudden forehead blow. After a few consecutive offenses, the punishment may get tougher for him for a while and he may get treated with a series of language tests and games.

LANGUAGE GAMES

An inmate gets involved in his first language game when answering the initial "are-you-a-grypsman?" question. Such games denote a variety of verbal activities. Argot duels and puzzles are verbal low-transaction-cost substitutes for physical fighting. Duels take place among grypsmen. Puzzles, along with little games, are typically used to test rookies and newbies. Sometimes grypsmen enter a duel or start a puzzle session as a form of sparring, just in order to keep their tongues sharp. When the cell climate is friendly, grypsmen and sometimes suckers exchange jokes or short funny stories. All duels, puzzles, and jokes must respect the rules of argot grammar.

The goal of a language duel is to show off and ridicule the opponent. If the winner respects the rules of argot grammar, a physical counterattack by the loser is interpreted as a mark of crude manners and dimmed intellect. The attacked grypsman will usually be left alone to defend himself, but the attacker's reputation will suffer. He may be classified as a primitive jumper unable to craft his response properly to circumstances and may become isolated in various cell activities. The fight reconstructed below followed a conflict over cheating in checkers. The parentheses show unacceptable variants of curses that might have been used in such context by an inexperienced curser, and which I will explain below.[8]

BOXER CONTRA SKULL

1. Skull, whore-your-mum, let your shit block your {fucking} anus!
2. I will fork you {fuck you} so you will shit out last year's meal.
3. I wish that your dick did not erect when you hit freedom. {in prison}
4. Before that, one of your balls {both balls} withers.
5. Hide yourself and your louse-covered balls in a redhead's pee-hole! {ass}
6. Sooner I will stick my dick in your cunt! {in your ass}
7. Before that my dick will pierce your auntie's ass! {skipping "auntie's"}
8. When I listen to that, my dick erects backward. {erects forward}
9. I stick my dick in your heart! {in your ass}
10. And I stick half of my dick {full dick} in your ass!

The duel was converted at that point into a passionate debate over whether the last curse was permissible, that is, what maximal proportion of a dick was allowed to (verbally) penetrate without being a blasphemy. Both fighters agreed finally that #10 should be withdrawn and that it could not be used outside of the relaxed climate of a prison hospital. They were deeply satisfied with their skill in wielding argot and fully aware of the audience's admiration. In fact, they closely approached the forbidden zone, but—except for the controversial #10—never crossed it. This is precisely the intention of a skillful argot fencer. In an unfriendly environment, the use of words added in {parentheses} would be likely to spark a violent confrontation. In the case of 1, 2, 6, 7, 9, and 10, the parenthetical words could be interpreted as an intention to fagotize the interlocutor. Modifications of 3, 4, 5, and 8 would suggest that he had already been fagotized.

It is easy to deduce from the recorded duel a few simple rules for reconciling complex curses with argot. One may wish anything upon a grypsman's "auntie" or threaten to perform all wild acts on his "cunt," the body part that a grypsman clearly does not possess.

Such strategies are risky, though. A local version of argot may be more rigid than one thinks and may disallow any apparent loopholes. Also, the mocked grypsman may claim an offense and try to spin an affair anyway. Fencing an argot duel is like playing with fire.

Language puzzles are similar to *little games* except for the lack of staging. The simplest question, applicable only to a rookie, asks him to make a choice:

Question: "So you have to entertain us now. What do you prefer, to meow like a cat or bark like a dog?"[9]

Obviously, both choices are wrong. A rookie should refuse the humiliating activity in as witty a way as he can. When he brags about his freedom connections, he may be asked:

Question: "Do you know Johnny Bardacha?"

Both positive and negative answers are incorrect, since "bardacha" is one of the prison names for the toilet bowl. A quick litany of questions may also be thrown at him at any moment to test his alertness. Immediate correct answers are required:

"Brick? Is hanging! Hay? Delivered! Girl friend? Fucked!" If the correct answers are not immediately forthcoming, the "brick" of a fist falls on a rookie's head, some of his hay (hair) is plucked out, or his bottom gets kicked.[10]

Other puzzles suggest an answer that automatically ridicules the respondent or that can easily be used for that purpose. The definition of the "correctness" of an answer is very broad. Any witty answer is appreciated. Such puzzles also have many uses, and grypsmen throw them at each other, not just rookies. The intention may be friendly or hostile.[11]

Question: "By mistake, a gynecologist looked in your eye instead of. . .?" The suggested answer—naming a different body part—is likely to violate an argot rule. The correct answer is based on a different understanding of the question and disregards the dangerous suggestion: "Optometrist is the guy who looks in your eye, not gynecologist."

Question: "What is the Russian word for 'matches'?" The right word is "Spiczki" which is pronounced in Polish as "from-a-pussy."

Such an answer is immediately followed by the triumphal declaration: "I am not asking where you came from."

In such cases, a good quip reversing the mockery is particularly appreciated. "So you need to see a gynecologist? Ask your mother for details" could be a good answer for the gynecologist question. A second best solution is a generic "acknowledgment of incompetence" that avoids answering the question directly: "I do not speak Russian" or "Women go to gynecologists." Such a strategy is routinely applied by expert grypsmen to all questions that seem tricky and to which they do not have a better immediate response.

For other puzzles, the default answer can be used as a generic response that reverses the mockery.

Question: "What is the difference between a woman and a beehive?" Default answer: "Stick your dick in a beehive and you will get the answer."

Question: "Why does a fart smell?" Default answer: "So you can enjoy it even when you go deaf."

Thus, if the question's format is "What is the difference between. . .," then a good answer is "If you do not know, then [*insert the default answer here*]." Asking a worn-out puzzle of this sort leads the joker to be self-mocked. A safe strategy with puzzles of unknown freshness is to target a rookie or to limit its circulation to closest friends. They will be more tolerant and appreciative of the effort when one's attempt at entertainment turns into a failure.

Some more aggressive puzzles involve supporting action and, like *Cable Car* described earlier, may well be classified as little games. A rookie or a sucker who scatters his belongings over the cell may be asked: "What is a difference between a closet and the jaruzel?" When he answers "I do not know," some of his clothes are thrown into the jaruzel. A similar fate meets his socks when he naively responds to the question: "I am doing laundry. Anybody want to add their socks?"

Telling jokes is clearly less risky than fighting a duel or exchanging puzzles. A good one sends the right message of quick wit and fluency in argot without taking an unnecessary risk of being mocked.

It invokes good feelings in the cell, and such a talent for making everybody better off at zero cost is highly valued. The best jokes are carefully collected in the memories of prison barbers, librarians, or corridormen and distributed among the cells as bonuses accompanying haircuts and books.

What would be told in Chicago as a "Polish joke," in the Polish jail is told as a "Soviet" or "policeman" joke. In addition, Russians, Germans, Czechs, Jews, prosecutors, priests, nuns, and above all, Polish and Soviet Communist leaders are mocked. Americans are often present in stories as the third parties, people of average cleverness but advanced technology. Thieves and grypsmen are kings. Sometimes, the joke's punchline may exploit the argot's rules. References to prison are frequent. Cursing is heavy. Blasphemies are punished. A sucker is not discouraged from telling jokes, provided that he can do it well.

To end the chapter, here is a small, representative selection. Unfortunately, many true little masterpieces are based on word games that are difficult to translate.[12]

What is the longest street in the world? It is Rakowiecka: Once you enter it you may only leave it after thirty years.

A Soviet scientist conducts an experiment with a fly. After tearing off a fly's leg, he puts her on the table and claps. The fly starts moving around frantically. He makes a note: "First leg detached, the fly moves." He tears off the second leg and records the effect. When he tears off the last leg and claps, the fly does not move anymore. He records: "Last leg detached, the fly lost hearing."

General Jaruzelski caught a goldfish. His first wish: Give me a big palace! No problem. His second wish: Give me twelve beautiful naked women! No problem. His last wish: I want the biggest dick in the world ready to play! Bang! The door opens and Brezhnev enters with a balalaika.

The final joke consists of a selection of answers to the doctor's routine question asked in different formats. Grypsmen often invest a lot of effort in order to engineer a supposedly spontaneous witty joke and then enjoy the effect like children. The answers listed below were worked out for one-time use in the relaxed atmosphere of hospital Cell 7.

> DOCTOR: How is your stool today?
> INMATE: Delicious! Want some?
> DOCTOR: Did you have your stool today?
> INMATE: I had some but it was stolen.
> DOCTOR: Was there stool today?
> INMATE: There was one in the morning but the guards moved it to a different cell.

CHAPTER SIX

Everyday Life

While initiation rituals, argot-speak, sex, and self-injury are the most dramatic aspects of prison behavior, everyday prison life is rich in repeatable interactions and produces numerous strategic dilemmas. Inmates trade goods and exchange grypses, form coalitions, tattoo, sing, play games, fight, steal from suckers, drink, and chat. An inmate's everyday performance influences his status and shapes his access to scarce goods. Once he establishes his credentials upon entering the cell, he can then enhance his welfare through trade, sharing agreements, creating and enjoying entertainment, or by violent exploitation. This chapter describes and analyzes most of the important categories of such interactions.

RANDOM WALK THROUGH THE CELL ARCHIPELAGO

The most stressful event in an inmate's everyday life is a *shift* to a new cell. It happens often. Prison personnel use shifts to neutralize supposed fuss-masters, eliminate the seeds of potentially bloody conflicts, or place a squealer with select inmates. A shift is announced suddenly: "Pack your stuff, shift," or an inmate may be taken for a shift from a walkplace or work. The frequency of my own "cell-to-cell random walk" was unusually high and averaged two shifts a month. My extra shifts to, from, and within prison hospital followed a successful faking of a complex sickness. A typical turnover is probably lower: rough estimates based on my data suggest a mean sojourn of six to eight weeks. The life of a quiet and healthy inmate is more stationary.

Shifts are stressful. A cell may be full of angry suckers. A newbie grypsman may then be forced to choose between life on the edge and hitting the gate with a stool to demand a transfer. Even in a grypsmen's cell, the local grypsmen may be hostile or just risk-averse and beat the newbie at entry in order to check whether he will squeal. A malicious fag may attack, calculating that fagotizing a newbie could strengthen his own position. For a sucker or fag, the dilemma is yet more fundamental. The harshness of lower-caste treatment varies enormously from cell to cell.

Inmates enter timidly or, more frequently, making lots of noise on an entry adrenaline boost. A newcomer may, in anticipation of the initial "are-you-a-grypsman?" question, strategically strike first. He may ask the question himself or respond with a query "And who is asking?" Yet more sophisticated strategies are applied. The following story describes one of many entries by one of my prison friends:[1]

THE ENTRY OF PRINCE

The guard shoved Prince deeper inside the cell and closed the gate. A few tattooed figures instantly surrounded the new inmate. "Are you . . ."—Prince interrupted the ritual question. "No, I am not a grypsman." The natives approached him closely. Prince took a blade out of his cuff and shouted crazily. "I am a sucker, cat, sucker-madman! Paragraph twenty-five. Leave me alone or—" he looked at the calm faces "I will slice you into pieces, grypsmen." Nobody moved. Prince quickly cut the skin on his left hand. Drops of blood marked the floor red. The grypsmen stepped back slowly. One of them made a decision. "Ok, you are a sucker but you are a tough-boy. You are kind, we are kind. Now, clean it up."

After telling the story, Prince showed me a few five-centimeter long scars on his forearm and explained. "You have to be careful not to cut a vein." As a junkie, Prince was doomed to be a sucker with no prospects for a *lift* to grypsman and had to look for other means of signaling his virtues. Upon entrance, he credibly demonstrated resistance to pain and the capacity to retaliate. The signal was strong enough to block potential repressions. Prince—as he himself explained—treated this demonstration as an action of last resort. He always tried to get a hint from a guard about what kind of cell he would be entering. On entry, he focused on detecting signals differentiating a tough grypsing cell from a less hostile one. When he entered my hospital cell, he was relaxed and did not signal in any way that he was a certified *cat*. He did not have to apply his painful method in the safe hospital environment.

Moczydlowski describes another strategic entry. A newbie "[u]pon arrival, in front of everybody else . . . touched his own sexual organs with both hands and then dipped his hands into a bowl of cottage cheese standing on a table by the door. He then stretched out his hands and, lightly shaking them, proceeded further into a cell, approaching each of the prisoners in turn."[2]

The inmate clearly communicated his familiarity with the purity classification. He tried to identify those inmates who became scared of his potential to fagotize and those who reacted indifferently. Assuming—rather plausibly—that inmates taken by surprise were reacting instinctively, he concluded that the scared ones were grypsmen and the others were suckers or fags. However, it cannot be inferred from the description what caste this newbie was actually from. He could well have been a sophisticated *ensign*, who tried to learn the cell's type before answering the sacramental question. Then, in a sucker cell, he could deny grypsing. In a grypsing cell, he could pretend to be a grypsman and buy a few weeks of peace before getting deciphered. While highly risky, such a strategy is used occasionally by entrants.

All strategic entries share simple common characteristics. A sophisticated newbie bypasses the ritual question on entry and tries to actively shape the interaction. His goal is to collect potentially valuable data and forcefully establish his credentials up front.

The high likelihood of a shift stimulates the active learning of the subculture and portable skills, such as story-telling, and networking with potentially powerful protectors. Seeking information about new inmates fuels secret communication. While making interactions "nasty, brutish, and short" in a Hobbesian way, frequent shifts also equalize inmates. They provide incentives to constrain conflicts and for even the momentary kings of the castle to treat their enemies decently. The roles may get reversed. Nobody is fully safe in the archipelago. The capricious prison Moiras could turn a king into a rat in a trice.

INFORMATION AND TRADE MARKETS

The main obstacle in the smooth functioning of markets for goods and information is costly and uncertain delivery. Communication and trade in jail are officially forbidden in virtually all their forms. Two kinds of information are most important for prisoners. First, supposed partners in crime are, by default, segregated in different cells, cellblocks, or even jails. Since sharing pretrial information about the investigation, and coordinating their testimonies, may be critical for their sentence, partners have strong incentives to communicate frequently. Second, grypses from other cells help to verify a newbie's caste membership. Thus, efficient communication channels help to decipher squealers or ensigns. Less crucially, the prison airwaves also carry numerous love letters and shout-out confessions, sentimental evening songs, hot debates on spinning affairs, business negotiations, and friendly chats.

The main technique for communicating is window-shouting. All window conversations are conducted in a similar format. Clarity and speed are all-important. Let's say that Melon wants to share the breaking interrogation news with his partner Chinese from a neighboring cellblock. He stands by the window. Then another grypsman momentarily stands by the gate's viewfinder and covers it with his head or shoulders.[3]

M: Chinese, report to window, Melon from Praga speaking!

C: Go-on, Melon, Chinese reporting.

M: Fucking King is selling us.

C: Melon?

M: Go-on!

C: Let's talk. Register to doctor on Wednesday.

M: Ok. Go-on!

C: Spin the affair and contact Bax. Fagotize the whore.

M: Ok, fagotize whore.

C: Ok.

M: Fall-down, fire!

Despite the brevity of the conversation, Melon achieved his objective. He contacted his partner, outlined the plan of action, and scheduled a meeting. The exchange was interrupted perhaps by a threatening guard's comment from behind the gate: "Temporarily arrested, stop this fucking communication." Or maybe the guard was in the mood for action and his arrival was announced by the hurried creaking of a key unlocking the gate. In such a case Melon and the protector of the viewfinder would rapidly jump toward the middle of the cell. They would feign innocence and act surprised by the sudden visit. Some bargaining along the lines of "Who, me? Chief, you are hearing voices" would follow with a likely outcome being a punitive communication report or a verbal reprimand if an offender is not identified. A mild collective punishment could also be applied to the entire cell.

Other communication techniques are less popular. Hand-alphabet is used in jails with transparent windows and the Morse alphabet is used for through-the-wall communication in the absence of more efficient channels. Ringing the sewage and water pipes or knocking on the wall sends a simple binary signal up or down indicating that a more effective channel of communication will convey a message or some goods soon. Political prisoners in the 1980s invented *telephone*, that is, talking through the toilet bowl when the water was pumped out. Since it required touching the interior of the jaruzel, telephone was explicitly forbidden by grypsmen's rules of behavior.

Unless a prison message can be shouted, knocked, or shown with hands, it must be physically delivered. The typical medium, *gryps*, a scrap of paper usually wrapped in protective welded plastic, is the size of a banknote and only slightly smaller than a pack of cigarettes or tea. No wonder that forbidden information circulates in jail through the same channels as smuggled goods. Such channels include diggers in walls and floors, *horses*—self-made window mechanisms, coordinated meetings at walkplaces or the physician's office, the paid services of corridormen or bribed guards, or the help of family members and lawyers.

When a newbie is a confirmed ensign or squealer, the holder of such information may shout it out through the window in order to warn grypsmen. In other circumstances, checking out a newbie is usually conducted with the help of grypses or other channels that are more discreet than window-shouting. The relevant information about an unknown newbie from the same prison is easily gathered during the joint walk with other inmates, during bathing sessions, via a short-distance gryps, or from a helpful grypsman corridorman. A same-prison newbie has little incentive to lie about his status. Checking out an unknown newbie from another prison is more difficult. When he declares himself a grypsman, he is asked for the names of well-known grypsmen who could testify on his behalf or for the names of his partners. The more names he knows, the better the chance that he will be cleared quickly. Next, local grypsmen with contacts in another prison send grypses asking for information. If there is another grypsman who was transferred from the same prison, he is consulted about the newbie. Grypsmen from the originating prison, upon learning where a dangerous sucker or fag was transferred, may also send a preventive warning. The entire process of checking the newbie out may take from six to eight weeks.

The possession of money, razors, knives and, perhaps surprisingly, tea, is prohibited by official rules. These goods, as well as cigarettes and food, are especially valuable. Other highly tradeable objects include gold chains, sweaters, shoes, pants, socks, vitamins, handmade prison souvenirs, or basic toiletries. Prices vary from prison to prison, and cellblock to cellblock. For less important goods, prices depend strongly on temporary fluctuations in supply and demand or emerge from some bargaining process. While many trades are simple barters, money, cigarettes, and sometimes match-box-sized packets of tea are used as currency.

The simplest means of trade is a *horse*, a small basket on a rope. A horse is placed outside of the window and lowered to the next level, where it is emptied by the lower-cell inmates and filled with their goods or messages. Easy to assemble and handle, the horse was reportedly used at Rakowiecka as early as the late 1940s. The downside is that its range is limited to cells in the same vertical cluster. It is also easy for guards to spot (see figure 6.1).

A more efficient, flexible, and safer channel than the horse is a *digger*, a 1–2 inch wide tunnel drilled in the wall with self-made tools. All cellblocks but one at the Rakowiecka and Bialoleka prisons are internally connected through a system of horizontal, and sometimes vertical, diggers. Given the limited resources that the personnel have at their disposal, the system is immune to destruction. Inmates, unlike guards, have vast reserves of time and strong incentives to work. In order to eliminate a digger, guards first have to find it, to remove everybody from both of the connected cells, get the bricklayer brigade, and keep the inmates away until the cement filling hardens. The operation consumes plenty of time and resources, while inmates only need about ten to fifteen man-hours to reconstruct the cemented digger. Occasionally, guards fill up diggers located at the center of the cellblock in order to disrupt trade on a particular floor. Typically, they restrict their activity to monitoring whether a digger's diameter remains within a safe range. The appearance of a large digger would compromise prison security and would trigger immediate action on the part of personnel.

A newcomer might find the circle of digging and discovery chaotic and arbitrary, but it is in fact a product of rational calculation on both sides. The payoffs generated by the constraints described above may be represented as the following simplified Digger Game. The inmate has three available strategies: do nothing, drill a small digger, drill a large digger. The guard can plaster over an existing digger or ignore it (see figure 6.2).

Figure 6.1. Methods of communication.
  Note: Clockwise from the top: telephone (used only by political prisoners);
pipe-ringing; digger; gryps; window-shouting; hand alphabet; horse.
Drawing by Mirek Andrzejewski, 2003.

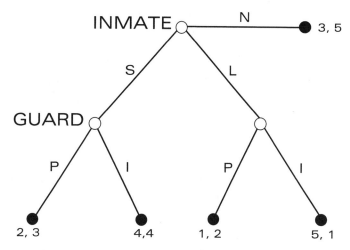

Figure 6.2. Digger.
  Note: *N*—do nothing; *S*—drill a small digger; *L*—drill a large digger;
P—plaster; *I*—ignore.

In the unique equilibrium of the Digger Game that is subgame perfect, the inmate and the guard tacitly cooperate. The inmate drills a small digger, while the guard plasters a large one and ignores a small one. This is approximately what happens at Rakowiecka. Guards essentially ignore the official rules because it is too costly to block or destroy every hole and instead only monitor the digger's size. Their plastering activity is reduced to the minimum required by their supervisors. Inmates use diggers for trade and the exchange of information and voluntarily put a cap on the digger's diameter. The Digger Game represents a variety of situations, when the enforcement of the official rules would be too costly or troublesome for the personnel. Under unusual circumstances, such as when women are placed in a cell adjacent to a men's cell, the parameters of the game may be significantly altered and the equilibrium may be disrupted. Chapter 7 discusses such a case in detail.

Before the system of diggers emerged, neighboring cells at Rakowiecka used to communicate with the Morse alphabet. The alphabet was written down on the walls of all cells and in scrapbooks. It was memorized by some inmates. In the 1980s it was still used in

Rakowiecka's elite and digger-less cellblock that hosted high-profile political and other prisoners.

Digger-mail and carefully packed goods are transported in long paper rolls. All cells subscribe to the invaluable communist newspaper *The People's Tribune*. Its usefulness for packaging is matched only by its importance as a substitute for toilet paper. The arrival of a package is announced by knocking on the wall. The roll is then quickly pushed through the digger and unpacked, or inserted into the next digger, by the next cell's grypsmen. The requirement of a quick response to a digger call is one of the most basic of grypsmen's behavioral rules. In barns, where the traffic is heavy, the duty grypsman responsible for weekly cell maintenance is also a digger-handler. His watch gets truly tiresome in the evening, with calls arriving every couple of minutes and rolls circulating furiously in all directions.

The digger system works especially well over short vertical distances. Trades with remote cells or with cells from another block or floor are usually executed with the help of corridormen, barbers, librarians or, less frequently, guards. The customary charge for all such services is usually equal to a hearty fraction of the transported goods. Goods and grypses are also smuggled by inmates themselves during meetings with family or lawyers, mass, interrogation, weekly baths, or walks.

Smuggling and frequent searches of the cell fuel the art of hiding objects. Top-secret grypses and small precious goods receive special treatment. Classic hideouts for a small package include one's bottom or throat, in the latter case with a strong thread attached to a tooth that enables withdrawal. Sometimes inmates sew small objects under their skin. Others swallow them and retrieve them in their next stool. Pickpockets, the masters of hiding, brag about stealthily inserting an object into the guard's pocket before search and then extracting it safely afterward. Guards respond by increasing the level of uncertainty. Family meetings, walks and other activities that create smuggling opportunities are announced at the very last moment, leaving inmates with as little time for contraband preparation as possible.

Uncertainty and high transaction costs hamper the smooth functioning of jail markets. Only fundamental goods such as cigarettes

TABLE 6.1.
Sample Prices of Goods and Services at Rakowiecka,
Bialoleka and Barczewo Prisons

Good or service	Price
1. Tea, 100g packet[a]	500 zl or 200 cigarettes
2. Tea, 100g packet[b]	700 zl
3. Large high-quality tattoo[a]	200–300 cigarettes
4. Bread figurine of Mickey Mouse, handcuffed[a]	40 cigarettes
5. Woman's portrait (from a photo)[c]	120 cigarettes
6. Naked-woman-and-flowers picture in a letter[c]	80 cigarettes
7. Copy of a scrapbook of a singer or tattooer[a]	400 cigarettes
8. One pubic hair from a woman[d]	one cigarette
9. Bread and fish cutlet[d]	one cigarette

Note: [a]Rakowiecka, 1985; [b]Bialoleka, 1985; [c]Barczewo, around 1973 (Niesiolowski 1989: 23, 140); [d]Rakowiecka, around 1979 (Trebicki 1988: 145); 1–6 are stable market prices; 7–9 are negotiated prices.

and tea have stable prices. For minor or luxurious goods, bargaining determines the price. Long interactions with many intermediaries introduce additional risk. Costly and time-consuming fraud happens from time to time. The high probability of a shift to another cell or prison virtually precludes credit. Nevertheless, given the constraints, the system works remarkably well. Basic goods remain in constant supply. Tea is almost always available in the desired quantity at a local market price. Fellow inmates are willing to offer it in barter while corridormen, often in cooperation with the guards, usually ask for money (see table 6.1).

COALITIONAL STRUCTURES AND RESOURCE-SHARING

As the most powerful inmates, elders capture a disproportionate share of goods through a combination of ransoms and compensations, relying on their capacity to spin and adjudicate affairs. Other inmates try their own tricks to increase their bundle. Experienced inmates routinely exaggerate their own altruism to put others in their debt. They noisily give away food they do not need, frequently refer to their past gifts in conversation, and avoid discussing the generosity of others.[4] However, the bulk of nonmarket exchange in a cell flows not from individuals' power of trickery but from cell coalitions.

Coalitions form to exploit gains from joint efforts or consumption. Two fundamental types of coalitions are *waferhouses* and *teahouses*, each motivated by the potential for a specific kind of gain. A typical waferhouse or teahouse consists of two to four grypsmen. There may be some overlap between the two structures or they may simply be identical. Tight coalitions of long-time *wafers* or *teamates* may also extend their cooperation into security. Strictly defensive or business-motivated coalitions may emerge as well, although they too are usually associated with waferhouse sharing.

A teahouse is a czajura-drinking partnership. Partners keep their own equipment, buy or "organize" tea, and jointly drink it. The coalition is motivated by the economies of scale that arise from group coordination as contrasted with solitary activity. Since tea is for all practical purposes a perfectly divisible and non-perishable good, the barriers to forming coalitions are low. Temporary, single-evening coalitions, with various groups contributing in proportion to their consumption, are quite frequent. In some cells, all grypsmen may be included regardless of their access to resources. Suckers may be allowed to participate with their own jars.

More important and less fluid are waferhouses. A waferhouse arises from the "intertemporal kielbasa allocation" problem. Since food parcels are brought by families directly to prisons, they typically include the most nutritious perishable products. Such products—"kielbasa"—deteriorate and decay quickly in a cell with no refrigerator. Before an inmate consumes even half of a six-pound parcel, the remainder may begin to stink. The market for perishable food is usually too small and imperfect to sell part of the decaying package at a decent price. Moreover, inmates from the package-owner's cell often play an attrition game with him: "you will give it away finally" against his hope "if I wait you will finally offer me a good price."

A waferhouse, a sharing arrangement with one or more cell-mates, looks like a good solution. Prisoners can ask their families to dis-coordinate their packages and then share their kielbasa over time. However, various problems of strategic timing immediately arise. Inmate X prefers to launch a waferhouse with Y after he consumed his own kielbasa and just before he expects Y to get his package. He may pose as superstitious. Joining a waferhouse during one's first week in a new cell—he may say—brings bad luck. In addition, the substantial probability of a shift introduces uncertainty over whether the next iteration will happen at all. When X expects the arrival of his package, he would be happy to terminate the agreement. Moreover, when bringing some food from a family meeting, he has an incentive to stuff himself on the spot or hide his kielbasa temporarily for secret consumption during the next meal. If he smokes and his partner does not, he has an incentive to use up his prison account money exclusively for cigarettes. All of these strategic subtleties motivate amazingly complex behavior.

Let us see this by analyzing the creation of a waferhouse and its redistribution of goods. Hats off, fellow game theorists. Meet Spaniard, a twenty-one-year-old high school dropout, pimp, and natural-born strategic genius rivaling Talleyrand. Always tops the cell's hierarchy. No family sends him parcels or feeds his account with money, but he smokes, eats, and drinks well.[5]

Student entered cell 6, his first regular cell, two hours after Spaniard. The cell hosted two career burglars, Max and Melon, an old, kind-hearted pickpocket Zgredzio, a hit-and-run taxidriver Taxidriver, and three country boys Kazik, Maniek, and Zurominiak. All inmates were grypsmen except for Student, still a rookie, and Zurominiak, who was suspended from grypsing until clarification of his status. Within three weeks, Spaniard had skillfully accumulated considerable power and resources.

During a few days of reconnaissance, Spaniard used Student's vitamins and Melon's connections with corridormen to organize an extra supply of jam and bread for the entire cell. This success became his claim to fame and the foundation of his power. Once the food brought by Student had been consumed, Spaniard announced that the rookie must be taught the rules of grypsmen. Student's initial performance was mixed. He ate his piece of chocolate while Melon farted at him, demanded a transfer to a political prison cell, and resisted using argot. Spaniard punished him severely for all of these offenses. Finally, Student carelessly shook hands with a sucker-corridorman. When another corridorman supposedly told Spaniard that there was a squealer in the cell, he announced that Student was the likely squealer and that the grypsmen should show him his place. While not declared a sucker, Student faced a long and painful America before he could join the grypsmen. The rigor included a number of harsh little games and a fagotization test. Spaniard himself conducted less risky tests and sent Maniek and Kazik to perform the potentially more violent games.

The common enemy—me—helped to convert the entire cell into a single waferhouse and consolidate Spaniard's leadership. Only Student and the suspended Zurominiak were excluded from the brotherhood. Soon, Zgredzio and Kazik received parcels from their families. The contents were divided equally among all of the wafers. Spaniard, always active, divided all of the portions precisely, enforcing perfect equality within the waferhouse. Under the circumstances, Zurominiak became a natural ally for Student. When Spaniard noticed their rapprochement, he immediately intervened and lifted Zurominiak to a full-status grypsman. The price for the lift was repressing Student, who by that time was practically immobilized on a stool by the window. He was routinely blocked from walking and discouraged from out-of-schedule defecating by a burning newspaper or a jar of jam thrown suddenly at his head.

Meanwhile, the leftovers from Zgredzio's and Kazik's parcels were consumed. After two days, Spaniard attacked Maniek, Kazik, Zgredzio, and Zurominiak and accused them of laziness and not contributing to the cell's welfare. Angrily, he declared the formation of a new four-person waferhouse including Max, Melon, and Taxidriver. The new coalition was minimum-winning: it included the minimal power just sufficient to control the cell's life. It monopolized the access to extra jam and bread, seized bunks, and granted itself priority when selecting clean underwear. During the next few days, Max and Taxidriver received their food parcels. The content was divided exclusively within the new waferhouse.

Spaniard attempted to repress Zurominiak, claiming that new facts regarding his toughness had been revealed. He also tried to set Maniek against him. To his surprise, they resisted and, with the other two grypsmen, formed a competing waferhouse, with Maniek as a dumb, but tough, leader. The newborn coalition also consisted of four members. While it was weaker than Spaniard's waferhouse, it had enough defensive power to discourage any further attacks. Student, the ninth inmate, remained outside both alliances.

Spaniard started courting Student, whose food package was scheduled to arrive soon. He claimed that the rookie's anticommunist adventures moved his imagination and were a sign that he might become a good grypsman after all. After initial failures, Student focused his mind on prison life and began to perform well. He avoided an ingenious beating trap during the "Blindman's Bluff" game and successfully defended his pants and boots. Once, during nightly chat, Spaniard provoked Student to "sociologically analyze" the power struggle in the cell. The accuracy of the ad hoc analysis shocked him and the other inmates. He ordered his wafers to stop repressing Student, started late-night teaching sessions, and even sympathized with Student against Maniek's aggression. He apparently developed some sense of pride from his socialization work and once told the rookie that "The lessons I taught you are for your own good. You will be grateful to me in a few months." In fact, the harsh lessons proved extremely helpful.

Spaniard's tactical cruelty ended most likely because he decided that the fast-learning Student might join the competing waferhouse and step on a fast track to becoming a full grypsman. Then he might even become the competing waferhouse's leader and a threat to Spaniard's power. Further repressions could trigger such an undesirable course of events. Spaniard's shaky four-man waferhouse would then face a united five-man opposition. A switch of a single grypsman or a shift to a different cell of even one of Spaniard's men could critically alter the balance of power. Such a scenario was plausible since Taxidriver disapproved of repressing Student and, since his hit-and-run victim was a secret police agent, he considered himself a political prisoner as well. Spaniard's resource-appropriating monopoly might then be destroyed and he could easily find himself an underdog.

Spaniard's brilliant performance depended on his risk-approving entrepreneurial attitude. Other inmates passively limited their activity to responses against well-defined threats. Spaniard proactively sought ways of enriching himself. For all his projects, he mobilized minimal coalitions necessary for their implementation and presented himself as a capable leader who provided public good. He actively fought against the formation of potentially threatening blocs. He skillfully deployed his vast subcultural experience and available information about when the packages would arrive. He also displayed patience and ingenuity, carefully executing his plans. Spaniard learned these skills and became socialized to his role during his miserable life at a camp for juvenile delinquents. The only opportunities to acquire resources open to him were through clever manipulation, stealing, and tricking others.

The study was terminated with Student's shift.

ARENAS OF ART AND ENTERTAINMENT

Jail art may be less sophisticated than freedom art but it is clearly less snobbish. It also encourages active participation since the artists are the audience. Inmate singers, bards, funnymen and, to a lesser extent, tattooers and artisans, all aspire to the safe role of court jester, since their accidental degradation would then make almost everybody else worse off. Security is the main motivation behind the prison art industry. The master of these jesters is the entire community of grypsmen.

Singing is the highest art. Fags sing on demand, but their forced performance is a miserable substitute for true art. Amateurs provide medium quality in-cell shows that are usually limited to three or four numbers per session. The best performers have a larger audience. They give through-the-window concerts as public goods to their own cellblock and perhaps a few neighboring cellblocks as well. Their services are free of charge. However, prison singers, like actors showered with flowers after a successful performance, get voluntary gifts of cigarettes, tea, or food from fellow inmates. Singing helps them to build reputation and recognition that are useful in case they are "shifted." The downside of window singing is the risk of being reported by the guards.

Themes of inmates' songs are quite different than those of conversations and stories. There are no vulgarisms, no sex, no references to anatomy, dirty physiology, or fags. They are sentimental. The recurring motifs in prison ballads include a brave young thief, lost youth, a deceitful sleuth, a court's error, a claim of innocence or a sense of guilt, romantic love and betrayal, the death of an unfaithful woman, a rendezvous with a hangman, and a freedom valued above life. Inmates sing about a " 'Yellow autumn leaf' . . . Crow Prison that is more black than crows, a canary that hums a melancholic prison song in his cage, a scared child who tells her mother that she dreamt about a lion, a brave inmate who does not fear fifteen years in prison, a corpse that fell on the green . . ."[6] Listen to these immortal and anonymous verses:[7]

> I remembered your eyes my love
> Separation erased them far away
> And a silent sound of handcuffs
> That a sleuth put on my hands
> You cried then silently dearest
> You thought I'm a hangman or rascal
> You looked with disdain in your eyes
> And now I yearn for you from behind bars

The artisanship of transforming the simple materials of the prison world into more valuable goods blossoms. All inmates gradually learn how to produce basic tools: a knife from a spoon, a tea-heater from razors, a towel-and-jar torch from a tin can and margarine. Substitute dice made of welded plastic bags, cards made from a parcel's carton, or bread-and-paper chess sets broaden the available entertainment options. Behind every product there is an elaborate manufacturing technology that inmates sometimes teach each other and sometimes enviously protect. More entrepreneurial types enter souvenir manufacturing: tiny figurines with handcuffs made of bread, straw caskets, photo frames, hand-painted postcards and envelopes. Many *faience-makers* hire bread chewers who provide them with a claylike substance for further processing and secretly import brushes and costly paints from freedom. While some of the souvenirs sell into the prison black market, the bulk of production is circulated further afield by corridormen and guards.

Painters and sketch artists illustrate love letters and reconstruct portraits from photos. Their art is usually associated with tattooing, by far the most sophisticated of prison crafts. While in the 1960s tattoos reflected grypsmen's social ranks, by 1985 they were valued almost exclusively for their aesthetic qualities. The signaling value of heavy tattooing was questioned by the more modern school of grypsman thought. These reformists mocked, rather than respected, overpainted men and emphasized the inconvenient public character of tattooing signals. Nevertheless, the market remained big enough to support both amateurs and professionals, who were paid in cigarettes, tea, or money. The best illustrators offered catalogs of pictures and bon mots, as well as multiple colors. A customary limited warranty against suppuration that could convert a lovely picture into a monstrous daub gave clients the right to a free correction.

Tattoos are rarely drawn freehand on a body. A picture or a calligraphic inscription is first sketched with a special pencil, imprinted on a moist cloth, and imprinted again on the skin. A set of three or more needles is bound together with thin thread. The best black pigment is usually made from the burned sole of a shoe, while the lower quality black, blue, or red one is made from the ink of a ballpoint pen. The thread binding the needles together also holds pigment. The motif is generated by pricking the skin with the needle set and inserting the pigment under the skin.

Tattoos may consist of pictures or noble epigrams. The most ambitious are multi-colored full-back images of the crucified Sorrowful Jesus, iconic portraits of the Virgin Mary, scenes involving the Holy Family, or monumental panoramas of medieval castles with knights. *Funnies* are strings of cartoon heroes, including most notably Disney's leading characters, such as Donald Duck and Mickey Mouse. *Patterns* denote small visual jokes, sentimental scenes, and thoughtful pictorial allegories. A pattern may depict a skull stabbed with a knife, a hangman's head and crossed axes, or a set including a bottle, cards, a knife, a gun and a woman entitled: THIS IS WHAT KILLED ME.[8] Naked women and girls are on an equal footing with devils, fire-breathing dragons, and hellish monsters as the most popular motifs. Prison professionals claim an ability to tattoo any living or inanimate pattern. One of the masters challenged by Student offered him for free a natural size portrait of Jacek Kuroń, a famously bald *Solidarity* activist. After careful consideration, the offer was politely declined.

Tattooing inscriptions promise DEATH TO COMMUNISTS (suckers, fags, or cops). Women's names, love declarations, and portraits are often the only traces of old fascinations and flames. Polish mixes with English and Latin, or a quasi-English or Latin lingo. A curious reader quickly learns that FEMINA VARIABILIS, NON OMNIS MORIAR and PER PEDES AD ASTRA. LASCIATE OGNI SPERANZA in the world of SLAVES and OUTLAWS—but also the world of SLAWES and OUTLOVES. Many grypsmen would kill for a good joke, not to mention sacrificing a scrap of their skin. An inmate may tattoo a rose on the glans crowning his penis and boastfully claim that "this rose will never wither." When guards started checking inmates' feet at bedtime, local grypsmen reacted by tattooing the soles of their feet with FUCK OFF YOU DIRTY DICK, IT'S CLEAN.[9] A slightly worn-out tattoo joke involves placing an announcement over the penis: ONLY FOR GENTLEMEN WITH A WHORE'S ASS.

Let's take a weekly shower with grypsman Skull, Student's chess buddy, a thoroughly illustrated man.[10] Take a look first at the half-inch high forehead of this remarkable life form. It asserts to those in doubt that HOMO SUM. His face, cheeks, neck, even his tongue are covered with little pictures, partially hidden under his beard. On his eyelids are two "sleeping" dots. On his neck are two red lips, as if left by a woman's kiss. Look at the spot around his upper right arm and chest. A pretty female is lying there with her legs modestly closed. Skull lifts his arm—and she lecherously spreads her legs wide apart. On his chest, there is a heart that is pierced with an arrow, surrounded by a proud declaration, I LOVE ONLY WOMEN. Fags, relinquish your hopes. The engraving on his lower belly encourages LADIES ONLY. An arrow shows the right direction for any "lady" who might possibly be confused. Above his penis, a few music notes from Chopin are put frivolously on the staff. Skull explains: it is just in case the "lady," enticed by the invitation, decided to "play his flute." On his left hand—a watch, on his right hand—bracelets and rings. On his feet are socks and a warning DO NOT TRAMPLE. His arms, mid-belly, and thighs are covered with aphorisms and pictures that would make Norman Rockwell green with envy.

Skull whistles joyfully, soaps his pictures with love, and turns back. On his left shoulder, a terrifying devil signals that Skull is a thief. LE DIABOLO IN PERSONA. His right shoulder displays the insignia of a one-star general. If not a bluff, this means twelve to fifteen years behind bars. An inscription around his neck refers to the future with a sad prediction DESTINED FOR HANGMAN. Below, a colossal black-and-red Statue of Liberty protects his back. This blurred and ugly picture must be ten to fifteen years old. On his right buttock, an Escher-like hand puts a tattoo on the right buttock of an inmate depicting a hand that puts a tattoo on the right buttock. . . . The lower back displays a simple and elegant THE END. The only tattoo-free part of his body is his left buttock (see figure 6.3).

Passing time begins in prison in the morning, around breakfast, with a relaxing amateurish psychoanalysis of a previous night's dreams. A bike represents a deceitful wife, shoes mean a change: a shift to another cell or to freedom, and n horses mean a sentence of n years behind bars. Puzzles, crosswords, and card games are among the cheapest time-fillers along with letter-reading and writing. Chess, checkers, and bridge are highly respected. Poker often generates conflicts. Stories are told of how young poker debtors were obliged to commit self-injury, possibly losing an eye or a testicle. Dominoes and dice quickly become boring and evolve into an activity of last resort. More ambitious types try to learn English, but give up quickly. The cell's attention may be caught for a moment when a con artist fools a rookie with one of his tricks. "Try to lick your own nose . . . Cannot? Wanna bet I can do that?"[11] Then he removes his upper denture, licks his nose, and collects a few smokes from the

Figure 6.3. "Skull": The illustrated man. Drawing by Mirek Andrzejewski, 2003.

dupe. From time to time, a prison bard may be asked to retell his epic poem or recite entire dramatized book chapters from memory. Since individual reading in a noisy and oxygen-scant regular cell quickly results in a headache, group reading saves inmates some mental power. Hopefully, all paragraphs worthy of a grypsman's attention—that is, erotic ones—are clearly marked in books by selfless predecessors. All of these activities help to kill time from breakfast to dinner, from dinner to walk, from walk to supper.

True quality time begins in prison around 6:00 P.M., after the evening muster. This is the day's high point, a long-awaited moment of happy revelry. But neither alcohol nor drugs fuel the party. The former is hardly available in prison and the latter is explicitly forbidden by grypsmen norms. Liquors made from toothpaste or varnish are popular only among old drunks. The delightful jail ambrosia, *czajura*, is an extraordinarily strong black tea infusion. Tea possession was officially forbidden in jails before the fall of communism, thus making drinking tea illegal and relegating trade to the prison black market.[12] If there is no fresh tea, one can re-brew, or even re-re-brew, the dregs. When there is no tea at all, the cell is gloomy and frightened suckers hide in corners.

When tea is available, it has to be brewed properly.[13]

RECIPE FOR GENUINE RAKOWIECKA JAIL CZAJURA (SERVES 4–6).

Take two razors or two rectangles cut out of a tin can, two matches, a strong cord and two long wires. Place razors opposite each other, with the matches inserted between them and fix everything tightly together with the cord. You have just constructed a high-power *heater*. Then attach the wires, or *antenna*—one wire to one razor. Pour two pints of water into a big pickle jar and place the heater in the water. Next turn on the light in your room, connect one wire to the room's radiator and the other one to the lightbulb. Be careful or you will be electrified. If you are not ready for the thrill of playing with 110 or 220V, first connect the wires and then turn the light on. Note: a blackout may follow. If you are successful, water will start boiling in 1–2 minutes. Then pour a cup of the lowest-quality black tea you can find in your neighborhood's most miserable grocery store, stir and leave it for 5–10 minutes. Serve in aluminum mugs or drink directly from the jar.

In regular cells, brewing tea is a notorious hide-and-seek game with the personnel. Guards try to surprise inmates with a sudden entry, and confiscate the tea and equipment. Inmates cover the viewfinder, listen to suspect corridor noises, learn how to hide devices rapidly and, most importantly, limit critical exposure to the few minutes necessary for brewing. The best defense is to buy tea from the guard's corridorman or to brew it exclusively after evening muster, when a guard cannot enter a cell without assistance. Since tea is precious, most cells limit brewing to the evenings. In barns, brewing is less frantic. Guards avoid entering large cells and let their business continue with little interference. In barns, wandering evening currents from tea brewing give electric shocks to careless climbers trying to reach their upper-level bunks. There, even floor nails are charged with electricity. One may also brew tea with a torch made from a can, a towel, and butter or other fat. This method is laborious, consumes valuable resources, and produces smoke, so that the gate must be temporarily sealed with newspaper. It is a fallback option, used when no heater or antenna is available or when a malicious or forgetful guard does not turn the light on in the evening. No method is too arduous to boil a good jar since "a pot of czajura, a strong smoke, and a fat fag" is a grypsman's cliche of happiness.

Perhaps enhanced by the comprehensiveness of prison deprivation, tea infusion stimulates the human organism like a light drug. Excited inmates slowly sip their czajura and, suddenly galvanized, jump-start story-telling: true ones or fairy tales. Inmates begin speculating, joking, and discussing the normative and positive aspects of prison life. They recall their masterfully executed criminal numbers, famous con artists who shared their prison bread, dignitaries and actresses they had burglarized, exotic prison customs and bloody riots, all fantastic adventures that Baron Münchausen would often find exaggerated. They spend hours debating whether "a horse with horseshoes can swim." But the magical worlds of ordinary freedom life return inevitably.

The overwhelming prison deprivation makes the memories of freedom incredibly vivid and sharp. "Only in prison does one live intensely. There, everything has a true taste. One tastes the sourness of raspberries and cherries, feels the burning sunrays on a beach, the sand under one's feet and the wet grass on mountain pastures. . . . Why does one have to find oneself in prison in order to admire the world?"[14]

Inmates focused on the tiniest of details carefully reconstruct tastes, smells, and images of freedom. They join their mental forces to protect their memories of things and places from fading away.

Pinpointing a specific Warsaw street, square, hotel, church, brothel, or movie theater suddenly becomes a matter of life and death. A taxi-driver nonchalantly beats the competition. "Where in Warsaw is there an intersection made of four streets with different names that looks like a regular two-street crossing?" Everybody is moved: the place is near a well-known square. Is that really there? This is where Student was caught during a demonstration by the communist special police ZOMO. "Tell us!" He tells them how ZOMO charged against the panicking crowds, breaking bones with ninety-centimeter-long Japanese clubs. The chain of associations develops furiously.[15]

Mention a restaurant, café, milk bar, beer kiosk, bakery, or pastry shop and it sparks a passionate analysis of tastes, tidbits, and treats. A fanciful manager of a communist fast-food chain used only names including "bar" for his outlets: Barbarian, Barracuda, Barometer, Barbara. "Where do you drink?—At bar Barbara!" chuckle grypsmen. He stole too much, bribed too little, and now manages his survival behind bars. A cook reveals his specialty and everybody joins him in praise of Good Polish Kielbasa. Wurst, ham sausage, headcheese, wiener, frankfurter, hunter, thin dry-smoked, and the queen of kielbasa, dried Krakowska. Even a hot-dog gets his share of nostalgia. Then a farmer timidly enters with his tale. He describes how to stuff a piglet, how to slaughter and disembowel him, clean the guts, and collect the blood for dark sausage.[16]

Hey! Everybody can tell his own story. As long as it is eye-opening, fast-paced, and witty. Just entered prison? Recount the latest Hollywood flick! Only American movies please. All other movies are too slow for grypsmen, too *silting* and *aproposing*. Story-telling goes on and on, an hour, two, three, until the light is turned off. Then erotic tales begin to dominate. This last hour belongs to the pimps (see also figure 7.1 in chapter 7).

FIGHTS AND EXPLOITATION

Perhaps surprisingly, bloody fights happen in Polish jails rather infrequently. Violence typically manifests itself in different forms. The numbers of cases of one-sided beatings of suckers and rookies, Fake Chicken, verbal and mimic duels, affairs, and self-injuries I observed were all in double digits. At the same time, I recorded only one case of a regular two-sided fight. This "relative peace" follows the self-sorting of inmates into "tougher" grypsmen and "softer" suckers. The informational value of the grypsmen-suckers division reduces uncertainty about an opponent's behavior and restricts the level of violence. While the common perception of prison is that it is a world of unpredictable and chaotic aggression, my experience suggests a picture of violence that is structured, calculated, limited, and to some extent predictable.

Two typical types of interactions are represented here by two games, one between two grypsmen and another between a grypsman and a sucker. Essentially, both games are One-Sided Chicken with either a weak or tough type excluded.

Consider first the decision problems faced by a potential grypsman attacker and a grypsman defender. A fight begins when the attacker irreversibly destroys the status quo and challenges the defender with a violent gesture. Usually, the attacker punches the defender, moves to the cell's center, and invites him with a shout: "Start!" or "Jump on the floor!" Such phrases are often jokingly exchanged among grypsmen as a form of friendly teasing. The defender may respond to the challenge and "jump on the floor" or surrender. A typical potentially violent interaction between two grypsmen is depicted by the game in figure 6.4.[17]

Let's analyze the payoffs in Grypsman Fight, with the status quo payoffs set at zero. Entering a fight imposes an expected cost on both players up front. While a grypsman may eventually win and be better off, the expected cost of fighting in a typical interaction is ex ante very high. Thus, both players prefer the status quo to both of them fighting. When defender surrenders, the attacker gets his highest possible payoff. This makes him better off than the status quo. However, the norms of grypsman subculture impose strong sanctions on those who surrender. Thus, the defender fears the fight less than the loss of prestige that would result from surrendering. Surrendering could be the first step to his degradation. Moreover,

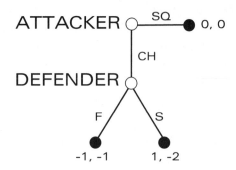

Figure 6.4. Grypsman fight.
Note: *SQ*—retain status quo, *CH*—challenge, *F*—fight, *S*—surrender.

he already passed similar tests while being a grypsman candidate and demonstrated his toughness. Thus, a typical defender prefers fighting to surrendering. In the unique Nash equilibrium of this game, a potential attacker sticks with the status quo, while a potential defender is ready to respond to a challenge by fighting.

The key factor behind the interaction modeled by Grypsman Fight is the attacker's expectation of tough resistance. The players' beliefs are firmly rooted in the common knowledge of grypsmen. First, the defender already demonstrated his toughness during his initiation tests. Second, during his socialization, the defender learned that the cost of avoiding a fight is large. Finally, he learned how to deal with intimidation and other tricks. These structural factors lower the incentives for a grypsman to attack another grypsman. Facing a potentially violent conflict, grypsmen prefer to curse each other. They may try to spin an affair or look for other means to sanction an opponent.

While a grypsman-defender is expected to be tough, a sucker-defender is expected to bow before aggression. Grypsmen rarely challenge suckers to fight. If they find it useful, they prefer to attack suddenly and beat the surprised victim. The challenge takes a slightly modified form: a grypsman steals a sucker's property or starts wearing his pants or boots. Then the sucker may accept the appropriation or defend his property. A fight gives him the only chance to win it back (see figure 6.5).

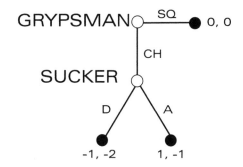

Figure 6.5. Exploitation of the sucker.
Note: *SQ*—retain status quo, *CH*—challenge, *D*—defend property with a fight, *A*—accept the theft.

The Exploitation of the Sucker game represents an interaction between a tough grypsman and a weak sucker. In the subgame perfect equilibrium, the grypsman challenges and the sucker accepts the theft. Naturally, in empirical situations the grypsman's estimates may be inaccurate and the sucker may be tougher than assumed. The great art is to make a correct estimate of the sucker's determination against a particular type of theft.

A fight in both games results from a mismatch of expectations or occurs when extraordinary factors critically affect the assumed payoffs. The only violent fight that I observed happened when a newbie grypsman stole the boots from a sucker-political prisoner. One morning on his way to trial, the grypsman put on the sucker's shoes instead of his own and later exchanged the stolen boots for his partner's. After returning, he told the sucker: "He needed your shoes for the trial and will return them to you in a few days. You wouldn't like him to face the judge in his dirty socks, whore-your-mother?" The sucker immediately hit him in the face and the somewhat surprised grypsmen returned the blow. A short but bloody fight resulted.[18]

The fight clearly resulted from a mismatch of expectations. Over the course of the day he had spent in the new cell, the newbie grypsman—a rather inexperienced fellow—had noted the sucker's conciliatory attitude and his voluntary cleaning of the jaruzel. Such behavior is typical for weak and scared suckers. However, the sucker was just transferred from a small, isolated cellblock hosting high-profile inmates. He had little experience with criminal prisoners and their customs, and acted according to his earlier everyday routines. As with most political prisoners, he turned out to be "tough," proactive, and ready to fight for his rights and property.

The treatment of suckers varies widely. The obvious and most important factor is the relative power of grypsmen in a cell. A sucker's social skills, his toughness, usefulness to cellmates, and the nature of his offense matter a lot as well. A tough, useful sucker may be declared "ok" or "harmless," be tolerated and admitted to various of the cell's social events. Political prisoners, some of whom refuse to join grypsmen on ethical grounds, but otherwise display values highly regarded by grypsmen, often enjoy a special status. Old and experienced suckers may be respected and are usually left alone. However, the power of the "sucker as a potential informer and weakling" stereotype among grypsmen is overwhelming and drives their behavior in many cases. When a grypsman or rookie is demoted to sucker, grypsmen immediately apply the stereotype to him as well. The importance of an inmate's earlier record rapidly decreases when a sucker's soul is "detected" in him.

In a cell with a grypsman majority, a weak and obedient sucker is systematically exploited and isolated from most of the cell's secret activities. He does not know what the local information channels are, where tea and brewing devices are hidden, who is going to send a gryps or when, or what happens in adjacent cells. He is under constant surveillance inside and outside the cell. When he writes a letter, a grypsman may snatch it away from him and read it loudly, to make sure that he is not writing a secret report to the administration. If he signs up to visit a doctor or a rehab, a grypsman signs up with him to monitor him as closely as possible. His scant belongings shrink over time. When he goes for a walk, a grypsman stays in the cell and carefully searches his property, often stealing some. The stolen goods are then immediately sent away from the cell through a digger or with the help of corridormen. If a sucker skips the walk, a grypsman stays with him. In cases of conflict, he is blocked from reaching the gate, where he could hit the button and ring for a guard.

Grypsmen master the skills necessary for controlling suckers through a combination of rewards, threats, and blunt violence. The most fundamental rule is to prevent suckers from coalescing, usually with a simple technique of "divide et impera." A sucker is promised better treatment or other benefits in exchange for punishing or otherwise repressing another sucker or a fag. Most skillful grypsmen, especially graduates of facilities for juvenile delinquents, develop amazing abilities to exploit even seemingly more powerful groups of inmates. One of my cellmates made a succinct point when confidently describing his power-handling skills: "Just throw Gierek, Jaruzelski, Walesa and Kuron [top communist dignitaries and *Solidarity* leaders] into my cell. In a week, I will have them sweeping the cell and bringing me my shoes in the morning."[19]

Suckers are intensely socialized to their inferior status. Former grypsmen know the rules and adjust to their new role in no time. Untrained rookie suckers usually try to speak argot and get punished every time they commit a verbal offense. They rarely get an explanation for their punishment. While a sucker's unintentional blasphemies cannot hurt grypsmen too much, he is punished in order to "know his place." After a few errors followed by punishment, a sucker usually limits speaking, hides in a cell's corner, and desperately tries to learn at least the basic argot-survival rules. Finally, even untrained suckers learn both basic argot vocabulary and how to avoid major blasphemies. However, their parlance is rarely cleansed of the subtle mistakes and self-blasphemies that grypsmen tolerate and do not correct.

While a sucker's life may be quite miserable, the purposeless offending or beating of a nonsquealing sucker is infrequent and many grypsmen disapprove of such behavior. The lowest no-rights no-respect social strata in prison is reserved for fags.

CHAPTER SEVEN

Sex, Flirtation, Love

Sexual desire in prison is initially suppressed by the overwhelming stress of being arrested. It returns slowly after a few weeks, hampered by the bromine and other sedatives that are generously dissolved in the coffee by the prison personnel. Some inmates try to avoid the compulsory consumption of drugs and drink tap water, but the tranquilizing effects weaken in a few months anyway. The first sign of a returning sexual drive may be the nightly pollution that leaves a white discharge on the penis in the morning. Old inmates often ask an embarrassed rookie: "Are you back to *cottage cheese* production?"[1] Then, they instruct him that he must take proper care of his penis. A failure to keep a grypsman's penis perfectly clean and cottage cheese-free is a serious sign of weakness. Such negligence is prohibited by the principles of hygiene. When accidentally detected by a cellmate's watchful eye or nose, it may become a first step to a grypsman's degradation.

The sexual tension in prison is amplified by the overall sense of deprivation. Inmates often feel pressured into a bold exploration of exotic avenues of sexual fulfillment and the acceptance of remote substitutes. They run the risk of being given an extra sentence. They believe in fairy tales of true love and undertake an almost inhuman effort in search of women. Unrealized sexual desires remain the principal preference-shaping forces in prison and are responsible for the biggest departures from the cool and time-consistent calculation typically displayed by most inmates.

MASTURBATION

Women are unavailable in prison. Sexually active fags are scarce and using their services involves risk. Moreover, inmates do not all find sex with a fag satisfactory. While some inmates working on farms try animal sodomy with pigs, lambs, cows, or hens, such sexual escapades are infrequent.[2] Thus, masturbation is clearly the most accessible and frequently practiced form of sexual fulfilment in prison.

The most striking feature of prison masturbation is that mature inmates, more or less conscientiously, accept a commitment to partial celibacy—between the morning wake-up call and evening go-to-bed bell—and enforce it collectively. Inmates recognize the potentially deadly effects of short-run intense pleasures and try to discipline themselves. Unconstrained masturbation is perceived as a harmful habit that may lead to addiction, degrading an inmate's alertness and leading to depression. All activities aimed at arousal, such as erotic letter writing or story-telling, are relegated to the late evening hours. There is no universal punishment code for breaking the rules, however. Restraint may be enforced both with passive jokes or with a more explicit punishment for one's attempts at masturbation, depending on local customs and tastes. Older inmates may commit to watching a youngster to prevent him from compulsive masturbation.[3] In some cells the only constraint may be an inmate's sense of shame. All those constraints are relaxed when inmates go to bed at night. This is the time when masturbation is allowed.

The default assumption is that, in fact, every inmate either masturbates before falling asleep or at least touches his penis accidentally during the night. Consequently, before morning his hands become temporarily untouchable for other inmates. This assumption drives two related behavioral rules regarding hand-shakes. First, a grypsman should clean his hands immediately after waking up and second, he is prohibited from shaking another grypsman's hand before the morning cleansing.

The lack of social constraints in solitary confinement cells is among the greatest fears of isolation. The increased sensual deprivation puts an inmate under strong pressure to overuse his primary source of stimulation. One can surrender to continuous temptation, stop rationing one's little joys, and "ride the horse to death."

In cells with the youngest inmates, the self-imposed restrictions are usually absent. There, impulsive desires take over reason. Frequent and desperate cries come from windows and from behind the gates: "Fuuuck! I want to fuuuck!" Youngsters do not restrain themselves as carefully as older inmates. A call "brother youngsters, let's ride our horses!" or "Polish cavalry—attack!" may start a *derby* even in the morning. This race of simultaneous group masturbation is won by whoever reaches orgasm first.

The typical masturbation pattern is less dramatic than the derby. After dinner and evening muster, during tea-chat or later, after everybody finds a place in bed or on the floor, erotic story-telling begins. Some contribute with tales of their women loved—or the more violent tell of rape—tales that inevitably culminate with a triumphal ". . . and then I nailed her!" Pimps are master erotic storytellers and they go well beyond the inhibited narratives of conventional love-making. Their stories are brutally explicit in their details and vocabulary, even by prison standards. They describe their harems, the colors and tastes of vaginas, the shapes of breasts, how their women suck penis, how they cry, how they serve their customers stereo "pussy-mouth" or quadro "pussy-ass-mouth-hand" (see figure 7.1).[4]

After the curfew is finally announced and eating is prohibited, after the light is turned off, and when the thrill of nighttime stories has evaporated, the cell quiets down. Life smolders under the dull grey blankets. The dim surfaces of the bunk and floor mattresses start waving rhythmically. At times a spring creaks, someone moans protractedly or silently whispers a woman's name. A sluggish shadow may get up and clumsily look for the lavatory. Then, mercifully, sleep comes.[5]

Figure 7.1. Tea and erotica. From the top: tea-brewing; typical tea-chat with erotic tales; no more tea. Drawing by Mirek Andrzejewski, 2003.

FAGS

In Polish prisons, the label of "fag" describes a bundle of social roles that are similar in their miserable social status but different in other important respects. A sexually *active* fag is an inmate who routinely assumes a passive role in homosexual intercourse. He is partially considered a substitute for a woman and partially a convenient masturbation device. The code strictly prohibits a grypsman from assuming a passive role in intercourse with a fag but permits using a fag for one's own sexual fulfillment. Thus, fag sex has little to do with homosexual sex: "Anyone who fucks actively is ok whatever he fucks. Pipes, fags and punks are exclusively those who let themselves be fucked. Simple as fucking. Those whore suckers think that we [grypsmen] are homos. Dick in their hearts."[6] Sex usually takes place at night, in a grypsman's bed, or in the lavatory. All interactions with active fags are shaped by the calculations about the benefits of fag sex and the costs associated with a longer sentence for prison rape. Grypsmen ingeniously try to minimize the risk of punishment while reaching their goals.

A fag may also be sexually *inactive*. Such a fag could have been active in the past and quit or he could simply have been fagotized for squealing. While the stigma is irremovable, a fag can build a reputation for inactivity by fierce defense against sexual assaults without his having to resort to heroism every time he is approached. A simple sexual deterrence strategy applied by some fags is to stop washing and bathing, in order to get a discouragingly bad smell.

Grypsmen abide by all of the basic fag norms regardless of the fag's status. Such norms restrict the fag's territory to the proximity of the jaruzel, ban him from sitting at the table and shaking hands with grypsmen, and otherwise require him to maintain a clear social distance from grypsmen. All fags bear feminine names and are referred to as "she." However, there is a great variance in the harshness of treatment experienced by fags.

Inactive fags are considered persona non grata in cells, especially when they are confirmed squealers. They destroy the cell's cohesion without returning any benefits. They are the lowest of pariahs and their default treatment is severe. Attitudes toward active fags depend on local factors as well as the length of interaction, since bonds of sympathy tend to evolve over time. Quite often a young, active, attractive, and humble fag is considered a valuable asset of the cell.

A maltreated fag may suffer frequent beatings and get strongly pressed to satisfy all grypsmen's fantasies. He may be forced to dress in a blanket-made skirt, dance the cancan, sing, perform fake strip-tease, and curse at himself. When grypsmen smoke, he may carry the ashtray around the cell. When they defecate, he may be in charge of wiping their bottoms. He must ask for permission to speak, go for a three-step cell walk, or defecate. His letters are cen-sored. He is often teased: "Want some butter?" or "Get butter ready!" which means that he should prepare for sexual service.

A gentle, nice, and attractive fag may be treated as a cell's mascot and enjoy some protection from grypsmen. He may get rewarded in cigarettes and other goods, often operating as a male prostitute. Moreover, he may generate benefits for the entire cell. Grypsmen from other cells may *swap* with the cell's regular dwellers in order to use the fag's services. Swaps usually happen during joint walks of cells when an inmate from cell A returns from the walk to cell B in place of another inmate from B. As an effect, the total number of inmates in each cell remains unchanged. Swaps break the everyday monotony of cell life. Guards either pretend or genuinely do not notice them. Occasionally, they may help inmates. In exchange for the fag's service, a visiting grypsman returns the favor by telling his best stories in the evening or bringing tea for everybody.[7]

In barns, a fag may serve as a personal mistress to a cell's fuss-master or to other grypsmen dignitaries. A personal mistress is protected by his owner and no other grypsman can use his services. In rare, but high-publicity cases, grypsmen may get emotionally attached to their mistresses or jealously compete for the favors of public fags. A mistress may "leave" his master for another powerful protector. Such a betrayal may start a violent fight and spin a chain of affairs.[8]

Some grypsmen do not enjoy homosexual intercourse, are reluc-tant to use a fag's service for moral reasons, or simply fear the conse-quences of a "fag trial." However, there is strong pressure from those who have tried it to get everybody involved. If a fag's service is used by all grypsmen in a cell, then the responsibility in a potential trial is dispersed. Once a grypsman breaks his moral scruples and starts enjoying fag sex, his security against potential charges improves with every new grypsman who joins. Health or other considerations associated with additional clientele do not matter much.

Grypsmen often brag about *blowing* a fag or fagotizing a rookie by force. In fact, most of them admit in private conversations that forced fagotization is too dangerous since it involves the threat of an extra rape sentence. While not frequent, trials against rapists do take place from time to time. A raped inmate faces mixed incentives when deciding whether to testify against his oppressors, and many rapes remain voluntarily concealed. The key consideration is that a victim cannot avoid getting back to prison and interacting with grypsmen. Effective protection by the personnel is an illusion. Every interaction with a grypsman may turn deadly for a fag who decides to testify, since the stigma of being a squealer who lengthened the sentences of other grypsmen mobilizes the harshest collective punishment. Nevertheless, the threat of a rape sentence provides grypsmen with serious incentives to limit forced fagotization.

Forced fagotization has another disadvantage. It rarely leads to the desired outcome, which is the voluntary provision of sexual services over time by a clean and attractive male "lady." Tales of malicious fags biting off penises in retaliation recur in grypsmen's scarytales. A weak and cooperative fag is a valuable resource, a tough fag is a liability. The point was well-made by a grypsman during a tea-chat: "You fagotize a tough fella and what? He fights, bites and makes a fuss. You fuck around instead of fucking in peace. He gets fucked up. You fuck a weakling gently and he starts fucking like a bunny and makes other fellas feel good. He even enjoys it after a while. Everybody is better off."[9]

A typical sexual fagotization, as described in chapter 3, involves exerting pressure on a rookie that puts him in a perverse dilemma. The smartest grypsmen provide incentives to activate a fag or to maintain a fag's activity with a similar mechanism (see figure 7.2).

The game of Fag's Carrot and Stick does not represent all of the intricacies of fag-grypsman interactions. However, it does illustrate the essential incentives that grypsmen provide fags in order to ob-

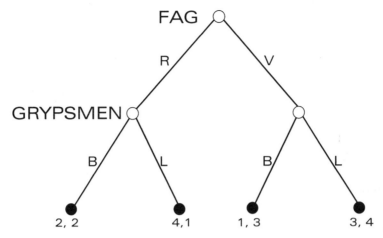

Figure 7.2. Fag's carrot and stick.
Note: R—refuse; *V*—volunteer; *B*—beat (punish); *L*—leave alone.

tain voluntary cooperation. A fag may volunteer with his sexual services or at least agree to serve without resorting to force, or he may refuse. In both cases, grypsmen may beat or otherwise punish him, or leave him alone. Unlike in the test of Fag-making, this time the nonperformance of sexual service is truly punished. The key fact about the fag's preferences is that he may be ready to voluntarily accept sexual services as a ransom paid for weaker repressions. This fact is revealed to grypsmen in the process of fag-making or similar tests. Thus, the fag prefers the outcome associated with (V, L) to (R, B). Once the fag is conditioned with consistent punishments for nonperformance and rewards for submission, he quickly learns the rules. In the unique subgame perfect equilibrium of the game, the fag volunteers his services. Grypsmen are determined to treat harshly an inactive, sloppy, or stubborn fag who refuses to submit to demands and give to a cooperating fag at least a temporary break.

The ingenious mechanism behind forcing a fag into action provides grypsmen with some insurance against potential charges. It helps them to exploit the fag and reduce the threat of punishment. The fag cannot claim that he was "raped" since he in fact volunteered his service. It also minimizes the use of force in the long run except for the short conditioning period. In addition, grypsmen often complain preventively to guards or rehabs about alleged fag's advances saying that "This bitch catches my balls and begs me to fuck her." They ask them to move the fag or themselves to another cell, a request doomed to be ignored. Such strategic complaints are presumed to help in substantiating the claim of voluntary sexual services in a possible future trial.

While questions about the purity status of a "fag's ass" are standard components of secret-knowledge exams, a typical fag intercourse is oral, not anal. A majority of experienced grypsmen with whom I chatted on patterns of sexual life acknowledged having oral intercourse with a fag, but few acknowledged having an anal intercourse. It is common knowledge among grypsmen that active fags in barns often experience stomach problems from swallowing large volumes of semen. Occasionally, a fag may masturbate grypsmen with his hands. In contrast to anal sex, oral sex, or hand sex do not leave any traces of physical violence.

Despite all the precautions, "fag trials" happen and result in long sentences. The grypsmen often babble in public about the benefits enjoyed compared to the total number of prison years charged: "Our fag was super. Well-worth the total of thirty-two prison years. . . . [Your] fag was cheaper. Since our fatherland gave you only thirty. . . . Bulldog, Sagan and company got the total of forty-three. . . . And their fag? Fifth category. Why such sentences? I guess they were blowing him and throwing up at his back."[10] Nevertheless, while grypsmen are reluctant to show signs of remorse, the bulk of their rare confessions deal with fag sentences. Many of those who received a sentence declare that they do not consider moments of fag sex worth the expected punishment. The peer pressure and temporary sexual tension push them toward decisions that they often regret after cooling down. One may hear the melancholic admission "I had more fags in my life than women."

Women

There are various categories of women in an inmate's life. Of those, mothers and sisters are relentless providers of food packages and prison-account money. Mothers and sisters are physiologically women but their shadowy existence does not stimulate inmates' imagination. Inmates love them in their own way but they rarely sing ballads or write poems about them. Their mailing addresses are hidden carefully since a typical inmate would not like to host a member of his prison club at home. A true woman, a woman as an object of desire, a woman that arouses passions, is not a mother or a sister.

Women from the freedom world who matter most are inmates' wives, girlfriends, mistresses, prostitutes from their harems, all those loved or exploited left beyond the prison walls. At first they visit inmates, cry, promise fidelity, and curse the stupidity of their men. Then the initially monthly or bimonthly meetings become less and less frequent and finally come to an end. Letters become scarcer, shorter, and more formal. A surprised inmate may get a court note and learn that he has just become divorced, since courts routinely grant wives a divorce in the absence of an imprisoned husband. Children slow the decay of relationships, but most inmates consider the eventual separation as inevitable anyway. Anticipating the sad outcome some inmates, after a few days of cooling down from the initial trauma of being arrested, offer their women terminal or temporary separations. They often regret their generosity afterward.

The high likelihood of separation is the probable source of an inmate's ambivalence toward women. This ambivalence mixes disdain with feelings of guilt. Although all women are considered to be bitches or whores at one moment, they can be miraculously transformed into beloved and dearest soulmates during passionate discussions. After receiving an affectionate letter or after a furtive petting session during a meeting with his wife, a moved inmate may declare that he will change his character and lifestyle. The unfaithful pledge fidelity. Thieves swear to give up crime "just after stealing a bike for my girl and a fur for my wife."[11] Dumped lovers return in selective recollections as angels abandoned in an incomprehensible moment of delusion. "At large women are not interesting, one loves and yearns only in a cell."[12] If inmates were able to keep their prison preferences after release, their pampered wives would never worry about their dedicated husbands.

After a year or two, good and bad memories alike fade away. Freedom women become faraway icons unable to stand up to their more real competitors. They return from time to time through a strayed postcard, painful anniversary, or inexplicable strike of nostalgia.

The more real women are female inmates. When female cells or cellblocks are located on the premises of a men's facility, prison love blossoms when the first lady enters her cell. The sexual deprivation of prisoners is so intense that a desire to somehow contact a woman may suppress all other activities and daily routines. The administrative rules separate the love birds physically, but the effective degrees of separation vary. Lovers may exchange verbal declarations, love letters, underwear and, much less frequently, enjoy limited physical stimulation. The administrative rules and system of control make ordinary sex virtually impossible.

The most available and most frequent form of interaction is window romance. The medium of communication is window-shouting, as described in chapter 6. Listen to a typical love dialogue:[13]

A: Bogdan?
B: Go-on!
A: I love you very much.
B: I love you too.
A: Would you like to be with me?
B: Yep.
A: Won't you forget me?
B: Never, Alka. I will remember and write you even after my trial.
A: Thank you, Bogdan. I love you very much.
B: Alka!
A: Go-on!
B: Do you have your photos?
A: I have one.
B: Only one?
A: Bogdan, I have one from the trial, but I do not look good.
B: Alka!
A: Go-on!
B: Can you bring me this photo?
A: I can, Bogdan, but how? Bogdan!

B: Go-on!
A: Are you going for a physical exam?
B: I am going on Tuesday to a dentist.
A: Bogdan!
B: Go-on!
A: I will give it to you on Tuesday.
B: Alka!
A: Go-on!
B: How will you give it to me?
A: I will throw it from the window, ok?
B: Ok.
A: Bogdan!
B: Go-on! [. . .]
A: Would you like a smoke?
B: Sure!

The exchange of tired phrases goes on and on, hour after hour, day after day. Guards often tolerate such harmless conversations and may even enjoy listening. Declarations are accompanied by material evidence of deep feelings: small amounts of tea, a cigarette, or a slice of kielbasa. Lovers sing popular folk songs or prison ballads of love and betrayal. Bogdan sends a letter written collectively by his cellmates with the help of past correspondence and catchy phrases recorded in scrapbooks. He may also hire a writer who will professionally handle his love affair for a pack of cigarettes per note. His love letter is next read loudly in Alka's cell. Then Alka may send a jointly written response to Bogdan, who will read it out loud to his buddies:[14]

My Kitty! . . . I am so sorry that you are already married. So am I out? Yes? Well. Tough luck. Since you have another one. But I still love you and will not stop loving you. I dream about meeting you and talking about our tragic affair. . . . Or perhaps you love me anyway? . . . I am so sorry that they will transport you to Białołęka in a few days. Won't you forget me? I will wait patiently. . . . Your departure will leave a vacuum and an unerasable scar in my memory. I do not know what is happening to me. I fell in love with you so deeply. . . . I am not enclosing the dill you asked me for. . . . I will give you everything when you get to know me better. . . . Your loving Pussy.

A mixture of laughter and serious discussions—"does she love him truly?"—ensue in Bogdan's cell. Or is the warm confession fully copied from her scrapbook? Inmates of both sexes would resist abandoning their illusions of true love even if they received their own letter, copied in extenso and sent back by mistake. But the desire for love is not the only motivating force. There are also clear material benefits from maintaining an open love affair. In addition to providing refreshing fun for an entire cell, it helps to exploit existing gains from intersex trade.

There are goods that, worthless in the hands of one sex, are highly valued among the opposite sex and serve as masturbation support. Among them are photos supposedly depicting the lovers, and *dill*, mentioned in the Pussy's letter, denoting female pubic hair or underwear with vaginal secretions. Worn out photos, dill, and other material proofs of love then circulate in the prison trade system and can be exchanged for tea and cigarettes. The strong smelling underwear must be tightly packed. Not all corridormen or fellow grypsmen agree to deliver such a perishable good. Thus, underwear dill is difficult to transfer. Pubic hair is easier to transport but its authenticity may be questioned. Even when a fresh load is supported by a love letter or other evidence, it may consist of the salesman's own pubic hair or a woman's armpit hair: "One [guy] came back from a meeting . . . with a bunch of locks in his hand. He said that he had just torn it from his wife's cunt. But he had no smoke, so he sold it. A cigarette per hair. Youngsters snatched all his stuff in no time. Then they held the locks to their noses with one hand—and jerked off with the other. The bunks were shaking in the evening. He sold it to twenty guys. Next day we took a bath. We look. . . . And this fucker's balls are shaved. He trimmed his balls and sold his own locks, not his woman's. We broke his backbone."[15]

The difficulties of distribution and authentication usually constrain the market for dill to the nearest neighborhood of female cells if such a cell is connected with male cells through a horizontal or vertical digger. The system of diggers allows for more direct and intimate sexual contacts. When women are placed in a cell adjacent to a male cell, guards often plaster old diggers. Then new diggers are pierced by zealous inmates almost immediately. They are usually broadened in order to allow for the passage of a hand and arm. A wider digger would catch the guards' attention and motivate them to fill it up. An arm-wide digger to a female cell serves its primary purpose well: it provides a medium for *digger-love*. Digger-loving inmates spend numerous evening and night hours at diggers chatting with their female lovers, exchanging gifts and, finally, masturbating each other.

Guards often tolerate digger-love since it gives them an upper hand in informal negotiations with inmates over more important matters. Since the physical contact through a digger is limited, there is no threat of pregnancy or other unwanted complications. Guards blackmail inmates with threats to fill the digger with mortar. Threats are repeated playfully during routine cell services: "Men, haven't you had enough? You know, I'll call bricklayers to fill it up." These are rare occasions when grypsmen show genuine humility and a readiness to negotiate with the personnel. Even those not involved in digger-sex understand and absolve their excited cellmates for flattering the guard and trying to entertain him with frivolous stories.

The personnel's tolerance ends when the threat of a full physical contact becomes real. In a barn, I witnessed the discovery of a female cell just below my cell through a narrow in-floor vertical digger. Letters and words of love-till-the-grave started traveling furiously up and down. The joint meeting of all cell grypsmen, in consultation with the women below, decided to broaden the meter-deep digger so that at least some inmates could slip down. The question was how to organize the project most efficiently, taking into account the fact that the guards were well aware of inmates' plans and controlled the digger's diameter on a daily basis.

The strategy finally adopted was based on a rapid acceleration plan. Over a couple of days, the digger was broadened slowly to give the guards the impression that progress was slow. On the appointed day, self-made rods and axes were prepared and hidden around the cell. After the evening inspections in both cells had been completed, rotating inmate brigades of grypsmen and suckers started

their frantic work in ten to fifteen-minute shifts. The work continued all night until the morning muster. Inmates saw excited women
downstairs gathered on the upper bunk below the digger, dancing
naked and catching falling debris into blankets. In the morning the
digger was much wider but still too narrow to let even the slimmest
man down or woman up.[16]

The project failed. In the morning, surprised and hardly believing their eyes, guards immediately called the bricklayer brigade.
The digger was filled with mortar and secured with a thick steel
plate. On the same day, the women downstairs were moved to another cell. The all-night digging race stopped short of becoming
another prison legend.

Full physical contact appears more often in tales than in inmates'
actual experience. No inmate asked by Student had ever had sex
with a woman in prison or met an inmate who credibly confessed
to such an experience. Fables of true sex mix with stories from the
mysterious female prison world: of dildos sewn from sheets and
filled with gruel, of complicated lesbian love-triangles, and of orgies
with guards. A recurring story describes a technology of rape conducted by women on male inmates.[17] In low-security prisons or in
places where contact between inmates of each sex is more likely, an
attractive female inmate may entice a male into foreplay in a remote
corner. Then a bunch of her less attractive accomplices would jump
out of a hideout, tie the erected penis at its bases in order to stop
the blood flow, and rape the victim at will.

CHAPTER EIGHT

Strategic Ailment

Inmates are known for developing "strategic ailments."[1] They swallow knives and bedsprings, cut their veins, insert needles in their hearts and eyes, and seek pneumonia or hepatitis. Political prisoners fight long wars of attrition with hunger strikes. Inmates faking mental illness may stay mute for months or set their bodies on fire. The sophistication of the strategies they employ varies from eating a rat in order to upset one's stomach to complex setups involving specialists from clinics and fake results of medical tests.

In strategic ailment, two main types of action are most popular. First, an inmate may deliberately affect his health through *self-injury* and mutilate himself. Usually, it is hard to make a typical self-injury appear to have been inflicted by someone else. In such cases, the fact of self-mutilation is common knowledge. In special cases, such as an intentional contraction of an infectious disease, the self-injury may be carefully concealed from the personnel. Second, an inmate may misrepresent the status of his health to the personnel through *faking* various visible or other symptoms of an illness. Usually, the fact of faking is kept secret. In mixed cases, faking may be combined with a self-mutilation that produces the desirable symptoms.[2]

Official prison statistics in Poland around 1980 recorded about 1,000–1,100 cases of self-injury per year.[3] This number is underestimated by an order of magnitude. It does not include concealed self-injuries (such as contracting an infectious disease), skillful faking that misled physicians, hunger strikes, actions that caused an illness "shorter than seven days," and suicide attempts. Moreover, the reported numbers were vulnerable to various statistical manipulations by prison personnel who had incentives to minimize them. In fact, virtually all inmates in regular cells contemplate self-injury or faking, analyze possible scenarios and their consequences, and discuss especially dramatic cases. The majority does not undertake any action, but a sizeable minority does. Both healthy and truly sick inmates play their own games. In the prison hospital, among about fifty inmates whom I met, only one patient was apparently not involved in any strategic ailment. That particular inmate had been paroled just before his hospitalization and the sudden illness had been delaying his release. All other inmates, including paralyzed and terminally ill cancer patients as well as those on their deathbed, were actively exaggerating their woes with more or less skillful faking or with self-injuries. It is safe to assume that if an inmate has a strong incentive to engage in strategic ailment, he will invest a lot of effort in order to learn all of the relevant facts and that he will attempt to do it.

Strategic ailment arises in the presence of a variety of social norms and organizational codes. Among them, the following are most prominent: (i) Humanitarian procedures and the presence of various agencies monitoring human rights or institutional performance; (ii) The high costs of taking care of sick inmates that provide incentives to the prosecutor to offer parole or suspended sentence; (iii) The necessity for the prison to be secure from epidemics or inmate revolts; (iv) Incentives provided by higher-level administration in order to reward personnel's performance, such as rewarding wardens for low mortality rates among inmates. As a consequence, an inmate who is considered "sick" can expect better treatment than a healthy one.

GOALS OF STRATEGIC AILMENT

A powerful weapon of the political prisoner is the hunger strike. It provides both plenty of time to mobilize public opinion and an opportunity to slowly increase the probability of irreversible damage. Political hunger strikers formulate clear demands against the prison administration or political regime that they contest. Criminal prisoners do not enjoy such a receptive audience. Their strategic ailment must appeal to more fundamental norms than those addressed by a political hunger striker. More effort and sacrifice are required of criminal prisoners to reach even the most modest of goals. Nevertheless, the strategic ailments of political and criminal prisoners share the same fundamental property: they are based on well-defined goals and a strong desire to look for an optimal course of action.

Thus, strategic ailment is seldom spontaneous. Typically, it is a complex project, executed according to a carefully designed plan. It often involves third parties who supply the necessary accessories, help to produce fake documentation, or assist with the procedure. The most skillful inmates work hard to minimize risk. In the words of a career criminal and master-faker: "It is no big deal to fill your stomach with iron junk and kick the bucket. The trick is to do no harm to yourself and get out of prison alive."[4] This perspective of an expert insider stands in stark contrast to official opinions formulated by many guards, higher prison personnel, and some of the prison researchers. Self-injury is sometimes labeled as a "pathological emotional reaction" to incarceration that is amplified by malicious hostility toward the administration: "The most frequent goal of [self-injury] is trouble-making and disturbing the personnel's routine work."[5] Such statements are at least partially motivated by the personnel's reluctance to acknowledge the failure of the penitentiary system to address inmates' problems without such costly actions.

Strategic ailment is neither malicious nor based on inexplicable premises. For a vast majority of inmates it is a pragmatic method leading to well-defined goals, and is considered as the best available action. For personnel or an external observer, the rewards at stake may seem small. Inmates may perceive the rewards differently or they may misrepresent their true goals. In all cases, the payoffs and risk involved are carefully analyzed. Among the numerous potential goals of a self-injurer or faker, the following are most frequent:

- Leaving a hostile environment: A sucker or fag may desire to leave the cell where he is maltreated. A grypsman may injure himself to prevent being placed in a hostile cell.
- Symbolic purification after accidental fagotization: A grypsman may respond with self-injury to his own accidental fagotization in order to send a signal to his peers that membership in their caste is extremely valuable to him.
- Enjoying the benefits of a hospital cell or room: An inmate may simply want to spend some time in the relatively comfortable environment of a prison hospital or to be transferred to a freedom hospital, perhaps with an escape plan in mind.
- Putting pressure on the prosecutor: An inmate may exercise pressure on the prosecutor to suspend the temporary arrest, to charge him with a lesser crime, or to suspend the sentence.
- Putting pressure on the Parole Committee: An inmate may exercise pressure on the decision-making body in order to receive parole.
- Meeting through coordination of self-injuries: Two or more grypsmen may coordinate self-injuries in order to meet in a hospital and discuss their testimonies or other important matters.

Asking self-injuring inmates directly about their goals brings unreliable answers. During my jail tenure, five self-injured inmates were interviewed by a psychologist or sociologist. All of the inmates first prepared for a couple of hours with their cellmates by discussing possible questions and the best—from their point of view—answers. Obviously, such answers were unreliable.

When inmates have less incentive to lie, their answers are more reliable. Thus, they declare self-injury to be a reasonably effective course of action in general. About 57 percent of inmates declared that they "sometimes," "often," or "always" met their goals through self-injury. In sharp contrast, 88 percent of inmates declared that writing a complaint "does not," or "rather does not," help them to settle their matters.[6] The inmates' conviction that they are successful does not necessarily imply that they are in fact successful. The question about the actual rate of success cannot be answered without complex data which are, of course, not available.

I do not argue that inmates are always successful in reaching their goals. Some inmates are indeed extremely successful, while some others lose their limbs or lives. In various cases a hypothetical well-informed observer would judge a plan of action as ex ante sensible. In other cases, he could predict ex ante that the planned self-injury will make an inmate worse off. Failure may result both from bad luck or a lack of expertise. The inmates' imagined models of how an organism responds to its stimuli and how institutions respond to their actions sometimes happen to be incompatible with basic medical or other knowledge.

My main argument of this chapter is weaker than the claim that inmates and their ailment projects are always effective. It says that virtually all inmates involved in strategic ailing have well-defined goals and patiently try to implement them, similar to political prisoners on a hunger strike. First, inmates attempt to optimize subject to their own subjective models and knowledge. Second, once they devise a plan, they execute it stubbornly, sometimes experiencing what to an observer may seem like insufferable pains. Third, in an environment encouraging strategic ailment, a great variety of techniques for faking and self-injury emerge that constitute a special part of the secret prison knowledge.

TECHNIQUES OF STRATEGIC AILMENT

Techniques of sophisticated self-injuries and faking are among the most secret of all prison secrets. While many grypsmen's norms recommend self-injuring or helping self-injured inmates under various circumstances, no norm deals with the transmission of know-how. Most inmates are familiar with a small part of this knowledge. Veterans talk about spectacular cases in public but pass on the know-how only selectively to the most trusted cellmates, outside of the quasi-formal setting of prison university (see figure 8.1).

Figure 8.1. Self-injuries. From the bottom left clockwise: nailing; injection; seesaw; cutting; swallow; torching; scald. Drawing by Mirek Andrzejewski, 2003.

MOST POPULAR TECHNIQUES AND ACCESSORIES OF STRATEGIC AILMENT[7]

anchor—a device made of sharpened wires and ballpen springs, and used in a self-injury through a *swallow*. An anchor wrapped in paper or bread is swallowed by an inmate. When the bread or paper is digested, the springs expand and make the withdrawal of the anchor with a bronchoscope impossible. If a thin thread is attached to an anchor, one may pull it up a little bit to make sure that the wires pierce the esophagus.

burning, torching—setting oneself on fire or otherwise causing body burns. A torcher usually uses floor polish or other liquid substances smuggled from freedom. A simple burn can be produced by scratching one's body and applying an onion compress.

Christmas tree, umbrella, cross—complex variants of an *anchor* that after spreading resemble a Christmas tree, umbrella, or cross.

contracting—contracting a communicable disease from another inmate, typically hepatitis A or B. Inmates drink or inject the blood of a hepatitis carrier, or eat rotten butter, fish, meat, etc., infected with a carrier's blood. Inmates often confuse hepatitis A, B and ordinary food poisoning, and apply contracting techniques that cannot produce the desired effect. A lighter form of contracting is catching a cold or pneumonia through a heavy workout and the subsequent exposure of one's body to cold temperatures. AIDS was nonexistent as a mass disease in Poland in the 1980s and inmates were unfamiliar with it.

cutting—cutting skin on one's arm (most typical), or belly, cheeks, or neck, often including veins, in order to initiate heavy bleeding. For a better visual effect, the blood may be pumped at a spectator or smeared over one's face or body. It may be swallowed in order to fake bloody vomiting.

diarrhea—drinking heavily salted water (one to two tablespoons per pint). It can be applied to support faking.

dusting—sprinkling a powdery substance into one's eye. A typical dusting uses pencil lead, powdered lightbulb glass, plaster, floor dirt, or toilet chlorine. It causes conjunctivitis, photophobia, and eye watering.

fever—faking fever or acquiring it through self-injury. Fever often accompanies injections and can supposedly be caused by injecting various substances into veins. A simple faking method is to bring one's own thermometer indicating high fever and swap it with the thermometer given by the nurse. In a routine defense, nurses secretly mark their thermometers or simultaneously apply two thermometers.

freaking—faking mental illness. It involves a variety of idiosyncratic techniques such as torching, pretending to be deaf and mute, random displays of aggression, and interacting with hallucinations.

hunger strike—a refusal to eat and/or drink over a period of time.

injection—injecting a harmful substance into one's vein, lungs, hand, leg, buttocks, or belly muscles in order to cause suppuration. A typical injection uses water with soap, saliva, urine, excrement, nicotine, tooth plaque, or milk. Injecting water with soap into the urethra causes exudations suggesting a sexually transmitted disease.

nail, nailing—inserting a sharp object into one's body, such as a needle in the eye's pupil, a nail, rod, or knife in the forehead or chest, or a needle in one's heart. An object sterilized with matches is typically inserted in an inmate's eye or forehead by his partner. *Nail* also denotes fixing one's scrotum to a stool or piercing one's cheek from inside with a tack and blowing air into the resulting hole that leads to a spectacular swelling of the cheek.

scald—spilling boiling water on one's leg or arm. The water is boiled with the czajura heater or towel-and-butter torches.

seesaw, hitting the line—an attempt, usually fake, to commit suicide by hanging on a tigerbar. A seesaw is conducted at night and is usually coordinated with another inmate, who waits a specified period of time and then cuts the suicide off the rope and alarms the guards. The trick is to time the rescue in such a way that it arrives when the inmate is already unconscious but not yet dead.

swallow—1. Swallowing a large object in order to keep it inside the intestinal tract. The most popular form of self-injury. In a swallow, an inmate usually inserts a metal object into his throat and jumps from a stool or a bunk on the floor. This procedure is repeated until the object moves sufficiently deeply into the intestinal tract. Typical swallows include knives, spoons, mattress springs, nails, wires, ballpen springs, thermometers, razors, and metal bucket handles. In some cases, objects can be withdrawn with the help of a bronchoscope. Often, a surgery is necessary. 2. A swallowed object. 3. Swallower—inmate who self-injured himself or herself with a swallow. See also *anchor, Christmas tree/umbrella/cross.*

tuberculosis—faking tuberculosis through inhaling powdered sugar, cocoa, or injecting sour milk into the lungs.

X-ray management—faking adverse changes in lungs or backbone, or an ulcer (called *rot*) on an X-ray picture. Relevant techniques include smearing powdered pencil lead over various body parts, inserting a piece of pencil graphite under the skin, or swallowing a piece of cotton soaked in ink or bread that contains pencil lead.

Various obscure techniques are sometimes explored by ailment entrepreneurs even if little evidence linking actions and effects is available. A ball from a ballpen supposedly can be inserted into a vein in order to simulate heart attack, or one may hope that an inexperienced physician takes an irradiated eye for a more serious dusting. If no tools are available, an inmate may hit a wall with his head or catch and eat a rat.

The popularity of various techniques is clearly related to the diagnostic potential of the prison health service, the medical education of a typical nurse and physician, the expected consequences for the future health of an inmate, and the likely effectiveness of the self-injury. The breakdown of officially recorded nonsuicidal self-injuries in Poland in the 1980s shows mostly swallows (54.5%) and cutting (27%), then nails (6.4%,) injections (4.8%), dustings (1.8%), and other types (5.4%). In addition, in 1980 there were 132 attempted suicides, about 15–30 of which resulted in death.[8]

Swallows emerged as the most popular self-injury technique simultaneously with the emergence of the grypsmen subculture in the late 1950s and early 1960s. A swallow is relatively easy to conduct since the accessories are widely available and it produces a threat to one's health that is easy to diagnose. Initially, swallows were fabulously effective. A surgery was routinely applied to a swallow and the swallower was released from jail almost automatically or received a shorter or suspended sentence.[9] When a high rate of success encouraged more swallows, prison physicians and administration responded with various counter-techniques. The technique itself evolved as well and its fascinating evolution deserves a closer look.

When the swallows became popular, two changes took place initially. Prison physicians learned to apply a bronchoscope in order to withdraw a swallow rather than to conduct surgery. They also established routine contacts with freedom hospitals in order to effectively use the limited number of available bronchoscopes. At about the same time, grypsmen invented a technique of pulling up the swallow just before the surgery was scheduled. A swallowed object was *put on haul*, that is, it was tied to a thin thread, then swallowed, and the thread was fastened to the inmate's tooth. Then, after the swallow had been diagnosed with an X-ray examination and the patient had been transferred to a prison or freedom hospital for surgery, he would pull up the haul and remove the swallow. He then had a chance to escape or he could simply enjoy a few days in a comfortable environment. His surgery would be cancelled at the last minute since the presurgery X-ray did not show anything.

Both innovations diminished the value and credibility of an ordinary swallow. Swallowers who refused to be treated by bronchoscope were often forced to submit to the procedure. Sometimes their treatment was deliberately delayed. In reaction, there appeared variants of an ordinary swallow restoring credibility with ingenious self-commitment mechanisms. In one variant, grypsmen allowed physicians to examine their teeth in order to make sure that their swallow was not on a haul. However, such an examination could not prevent the use of a bronchoscope. Grypsmen who wanted surgery invented anchors, Christmas trees, crosses, or umbrellas and other devices signaling commitment (see descriptions given previously). Once swallowed, these devices became fixed to the wall of the esophagus. This made pulling the swallow out with a haul or with a bronchoscope impossible. Such a *sharp swallow* could easily be identified with an X-ray examination and the only method of removal was surgery.

The invention of sharp swallows resulted in modifications of other techniques of self-injury, such as anchored needles inserted in eyes or sharp anchors inserted in the penis's urethra. However, another grypsmen invention soon eroded the credibility of a sharp swallow. Self-commitment could be faked with a *fake anchor.* The sharp ends of a regular anchor were put into small plastic beads made of a melted toothbrush handle or soap-box. The X-ray showed the metal anchor but did not show the plastic, suggesting a sharp swallow. In fact, the swallow could be pulled out with a cleverly hidden haul.

All new techniques that grypsmen gradually developed over time either tried to restore the credibility damaged by the previous innovation or tried to fake the so-far credible technique. In the latest iteration, the most advanced technique enabled pulling out a fake sharp swallow without a haul attached to a tooth.

How to Pull Out a Fake Sharp Swallow?

Let's say that you swallowed a fake anchor or cross. The X-ray examination will show a sharp swallow. Let the prison physician carefully examine your mouth and throat. You will be transferred to a prison or freedom hospital and prepared for surgery. On the eve of the operation, assemble a *virtual haul*. It consists of two components. First, you need a couple of buttons. If your grey hospital pajama has none, you may get or buy a few from your cellmates. Second, you need a two-yard long thread. Again, use your prison pajama to extract thread. If you have enough thread, weave three or four pieces into one strong rope. Fix buttons to the thread in 5–6 inch intervals, starting at its end. Then gradually swallow the buttons with the thread—but not entirely! The unbuttoned end must stick out of your mouth. Swallowing takes a while. Vomiting is a typical reaction if you go too fast. In such a case, wash the haul, rest a few minutes, and try again. When you successfully swallow the haul, put a blanket on the floor and start flipping somersaults. Relax: you can do it on the floor instead of in the air. After 10–15 minutes, the buttons will entangle the swallow since you had bent the anchor wires appropriately before you swallowed it. Carefully pull the anchor out. If you are not successful at your first attempt, try again. On the day of scheduled surgery, the X-ray examination will show nothing. You may tell the furious and astounded surgeon that "your stomach dissolves iron," a running joke among veteran swallowers.[10]

Cases of Self-Injury

A self-injury may send a symbolic signal to someone or it may aim at generating pragmatic benefits for the self-injurer.[11] On entering a new cell, as described in chapter 6, Prince lightly self-injured himself in order to send a credible signal of toughness to his new cellmates. He did not expect any immediate material reward for his action. Instead, his goal was to establish the right reputation in the eyes of other inmates. In similar cases, the "benefits" are granted exclusively by some "benefactor," the party who evaluates and acts in response to the self-injurer's behavior. Committing self-injury sends meaningful information to the benefactor, or *symbolically sig-nals* to him the type of a self-injurer. The benefactor takes the next step and uses his discretion in deciding how to treat the signaler. The benefits are not a direct consequence of the self-injury.

In the case of a *pragmatic* self-injury, while there may be a deci-sion-making benefactor as well, the decision is an automatic conse-quence of the act. The benefactor's role is only technical. An exam-ple is a guard's decision to call a doctor when he discovers a suicide attempt. While one can imagine a guard who tries to cover up the suicide or delay a physician's arrival, it is safe to assume that a typical guard acts as an "automatic alarm device" that detects self-injury. Such cases do not involve meaningful interactions among the vari-ous players, but rather a complex optimization problem being worked out by a single decision-maker.

Finally, one can identify *mixed pragmatic-signaling* cases, when both kinds of benefits are substantial.

One may notice that in signaling self-injuries, some "material" benefits that follow a benefactor's action are also ultimately present. The distinction introduced above relies on the fact that in the sec-ond case the self-injurer can effectively ignore the presence of an-other player. He can assume that his actions immediately produce certain consequences and that he faces a decision-making problem rather than a game. Thus, this distinction obviously depends on how the self-injurer mentally represents the situation. However, such dependence does not lead to ambiguity in our classification. Virtually all cases of self-injury are pretty easy to classify once a self-injurer's intentions are properly decoded.

Pure Signaling Motives: "The Cry of Desperation"

Self-injuries as a form of signaling are common in prison. Mal-treated suckers and fags, or grypsmen in sucker-dominated cells often commit self-injuries in order to force the administration to move them to a more friendly cell. A self-injury by a grypsman fagotized by a malicious sucker carries the message: "my life outside of the grypsmen cast is worthless, the fagotization was an accident, I am tough and do not deserve degradation." Outside of prison, the goal of a teenager's suicide attempt may be to signal his or her desperation to relatives. In all of these cases, self-injury is the action of last resort. It follows one's conviction that such a costly method is the best—or perhaps the only—available way to signal one's determination, desperation, or strength of preferences.

The "Cry of Desperation" game provides a formal representation of one of the forms of the phenomenon described above. In the game, a maliciously fagotized grypsman faces the choice of whether to self-injure himself. Then the elders must decide whether to degrade the grypsman to a lower caste or spare him. The grypsman may strongly care about his caste membership (he is called "loyal" to his caste) or may put a low valuation on it (he is called "disloyal"). For both types of grypsmen, status quo with no self-injury is the best outcome, while degradation combined with self-injury is the worst outcome. Preferences over the remaining two outcomes differ. A loyal type prefers self-injury that saves him from degradation over degradation without self-injury, while the disloyal type's preferences are the reverse. For the elders, sparing a loyal type and degrading a disloyal type provide the highest payoff, while sparing a disloyal type and degrading a loyal type provides the lowest payoff. The proportions of both types in the population are positive, that is, $0<p<1$, and known to all players (see figure 8.2).[12]

Two types of equilibria are possible.[13] In both equilibria, the disloyal type always avoids self-injury since such an action always brings him a higher payoff than self-injuring. The loyal type and the elders may behave in a variety of ways in equilibrium.

In the first equilibrium, when they believe that the proportion of disloyal types is sufficiently high, the elders degrade the grypsman regardless of his actions, and no type of grypsman injures himself. When the proportion of disloyal types falls below the critical level, a different equilibrium emerges, in which the elders never degrade and nobody self-injures. At the critical level, the elders are indifferent between their two strategies.[14] In such a *pooling equilibrium*, the elders' strategy is "stiff": They either punish or forgive everybody. In both cases, no incentives exist for a grypsman to send a costly signal.

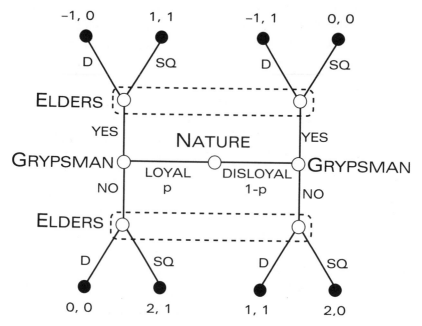

Figure 8.2. Cry of desperation.
Note: *LOYAL* (*DISLOYAL*)—Grypsman with a high (low) valuation of his
caste membership; *YES* (*NO*)—the Grypsman's decision whether to commit a self-
injury or not; *D* (*SQ*)—decision of the Elders whether to degrade the Grypsman
to a sucker or maintain his status quo caste membership.

More interesting is the second, *separating equilibrium*. The elders forgive all those who commit self-injury and degrade all those
who do not self-injure; the loyal type self-injures and the disloyal
type does not self-injure. This is an instance of a more sophisticated
subculture, in which signals are properly decoded by the elders. In
such an equilibrium, self-injury is a rational reaction for the loyal
type. A loyal grypsman responding to the elders' strategy in a separating equilibrium is strictly better off when he self-injures.

Strategic situations similar to the "Cry of Desperation" game
often appear when no clear "material" motive behind a self-injury
can be identified. A closer examination of a player's mental state
may reveal his desire to send a signal as motivating his decision. I
met only one grypsman who appeared not to have a clear motive

behind his self-injury. *Devil* was a slightly retarded inmate, who scalded his legs with boiling water "to show his solidarity with all grypsmen." Other grypsmen considered his self-injury meaningless but also provided him with some claim to respect. After a few days of friendly conversations and an invitation to a tea party, Devil finally confessed his true motive. In his previous cell, grypsmen poked fun at him even though he was a grypsman himself. He became afraid that they may degrade him during a longer stretch of boredom. "Look Student, whore-your-mum, maybe I am not terribly smart but I am a true grypsman. And I showed them." Apparently, his scald was a preventive measure. He signaled to potential curse-holders that there was a limit to the jokes he was willing to tolerate and that he was not afraid to bear a very high cost in order to defend his caste membership.

Cries of desperation may take place in more complex settings. They appear frequently when inmates are shifted to new cells. The prison administration is restricted in where it can place inmates by the prosecutor's demand to separate inmates charged in the same case, and by the rules for planting squealers. A shift of an inmate is also pretty costly in terms of the resources it consumes, and while shifts happen often, they rarely follow an inmate's request. A self-injuring inmate signals to the administration that he is determined to impose an even greater cost on them than that of a shift. Moreover, once an inmate leaves his cell and goes to a hospital cell, the cost of transferring him back to the old cell becomes about the same as placing him in a new cell. No wonder that self-injury became an extremely effective means for a strongly motivated inmate in forcing the administration to shift. The following story illustrates a typical case of the late 1960s and early 1970s when the prison administration tried to force grypsmen to abandon their caste.

A new grypsman Grzesiek [was transferred to our prison] . . . This whore rehab checks his file and tells him: "Cell 15." And 15 was a suckers' cell, which Grzesiek knew from a gryps. And that they will try to fagotize him. . . . So he tells the whore: "No! Or I will ride on my veins!" And he shows: in one hand a knife, in the other a razor, and in his mouth a sharp anchor, ready to swallow. The whore rehab repeats: "Fifteen!"

Then Grzesiek . . . hits the window pane with his hands. He is covered with blood and the whore laughs at him: "Not enough. Show more and you will go to those grypsmen." So Grzesiek hits a second pane. Third. Fourth. . . . thirty panes smashed . . . and he faints . . . eighty meters of floor covered with his blood . . . "OK! You are a tough guy. You can go to your grypsmen"—this whore rehab tells him finally."[15]

The display of toughness convinced the rehab that placing Grzesiek with nongrypsmen would be prohibitively costly. The grypsman's reaction depicted above was hardly unusual. The high frequency of similar reactions and the associated high costs resulted in the abandonment of the administration's policy of forced "degrypsing."

Pure Pragmatic Motives

The most common pragmatic motive behind self-injury is change: a change of surroundings to a more comfortable health room or hospital environment. In an extreme case, Cat, the inmate who mastered the technique for pulling out a fake sharp swallow described earlier, used his skills in order to wander from prison to prison and hospital to hospital. Even after applying the trick a few times, he was still able to persuade the guards and prison nurses that he had a serious illness and subsequently mislead the surgeons. In his "prison wandering" he exploited the poor integration of databases with inmate records in various prisons.

An interesting category of pragmatic self-injuries evolved in response to the prison authorities' attempts to prevent jail inmates from communicating. Two or more inmates may coordinate their self-injuries and meet in the prison's health center in order to discuss an ongoing affair or other current matters.[16] In a less costly, though less effective, version of such a coordinated meeting two inmates will simultaneously make an appointment with a doctor or a dentist and hope that they will meet in the doctor's waiting room.

A more sophisticated version of coordinated self-injuries exploits authorities' predictable allocation of sick inmates. It arises from the separation of partners in crime prior to their trial and the fact that the inmates have no right to contact a lawyer. Strongly motivated to communicate directly, the inmates take advantage of the fact that the administration keeps records enabling them to isolate partners only within a given prison. It loses its control over the allocation of sick inmates. Since the number of specialized hospital departments is small, one can reliably predict where the specific case of self-injury will be treated. Thus, partners in crime from different cellblocks or prisons may coordinate their self-injuries with grypses and be simultaneously transferred to the same specialized hospital department of a different prison. Once on the same cellblock, they can easily discuss the details of their defense strategy at the walk-place or with a digger or by shouting messages.[17]

Another category of pragmatic self-injuries involves contracting a contagious disease, typically hepatitis A or B. One of the Rakowiecka prison fuss-masters acquired access to an inmate with hepatitis-infected blood. In consultation with Student, the fuss-master revealed that his sentence was seven years, over three of which he had already served. As a well-known leader of grypsmen, he had no chance for good-behavior parole. He worked out the idea of contracting hepatitis long ago and waited until mid-sentence in order to increase his chance of getting a parole due to sickness. His trade-off involved contracting hepatitis in exchange for about 3.5 years off his sentence. His decision problem was that he did not know whether he should eat or inject the infected blood. The advice Student offered him was to combine both actions: In order to maximize his chances, the fuss-master should both eat and inject the infected blood.[18]

Mixed Signaling and Pragmatic Motives

Self-injurers are usually transferred to the prison's health room or hospital and automatically enjoy the benefits of a friendlier environment. While such pragmatic benefits may be considered negligible in the cases of signaling, in other cases they may be perceived as roughly on par.

Mixed motives may appear in the hunger strike of a political prisoner. While in some cases the strike may be a pure signaling game of attrition with the guards and warden to send a message about an inmate's toughness, in other cases a high-profile political prisoner may initiate a hunger strike with the immediate pragmatic benefits of external publicity in mind. A hunger strike may also stop an inmate's transfer to another prison or make his participation in a trial impossible.

The delay of a trial is a very popular motive for a mixed self-injury among criminal prisoners. An inmate commits self-injury on the eve of the scheduled trial. He is immediately taken to a hospital. There is not enough time to notify the judges, lawyers, prosecutors, witnesses, or to cancel the possible transportation of co-defendants from other prisons. Without the main defendant present, the trial cannot proceed. Thus, when the court assembles on the next day, the session is cancelled and the next trial date is usually scheduled in six to eight weeks. At that time another self-injury may be committed. A defendant gains in two different ways. First, the trial is delayed. Inmates believe, and with good reason, that the later a trial takes place, the shorter an expected sentence is and the more likely that the sentence will be suspended. Second, the defendant sends a signal to the prosecutor that he is capable of imposing heavy costs on him or her. The expected reaction of the prosecutor is to charge the defendant with a lesser crime, with lower *brackets*, in other words, shorter minimum and maximum sentences.

I recorded a fascinating case of a mixed rotating self-injury during my ten-week tenure at the prison's surgical department.[19] Wojtek and Jacek were leaders of a gang that robbed cars and gas stations. When I entered the hospital, Wojtek was about to leave after a saliva injection in his cheek. After a few weeks, Jacek came to the hospital with a scald on both legs. When I was leaving the surgical department, I met Wojtek again in the hospital's hall. He was waiting for admission with a knee injection.

Wojtek and Jacek's goal was to delay the trial and, more importantly, to impose a high cost on the prosecutor. Their brackets were [10, 15] and they expected twelve- to thirteen-year sentences. They aimed at a more favorable sentence, with the brackets of [5, 10]. Most of Wojtek and Jacek's prison activity was organized around coordinating self-injuries and exchanging messages on a daily basis via window-shouting and grypses. They were determined to rotate their self-injury until the prosecutor changed the charges. The prosecutor was well aware of their goals. After the third iteration, she signaled a willingness to compromise. Then, after receiving the expected eight-year sentence, they planned to study and behave faultlessly in prison in order to get parole. Because they were youngsters at the time they committed the crime, they would be eligible for parole after four years.

CASES OF FAKING

While faking an illness may use one or more procedures similar to those described in the list given previously, different cases are usually dissimilar. Any model that would try to represent faking would have to focus on specific cases and would carry little general value. Thus, there is a good reason to abandon formalism here and focus on key empirical regularities. Below, I discuss in more detail a few interesting case studies.

One may fake (i) visible "hard" symptoms, that is, symptoms based on the results of standard tests, such as fever or the presence of blood in the urine; (ii) visible "soft" symptoms, that is, symptoms produced with acting; (iii) supporting paperwork from specialists, based on the results of specialized tests. Individual faking projects are usually designed around one of these three strategies. They are typically supported by more or less serious self-injuries.

Experienced fakers are always ready to offer a few generic helpful rules of thumb to a novice: do not talk too much, do not pretend that you know too much, do not go for walks, do not eat too much. However, the success of faking depends on a number of variables that the inmate has little control over, such as the local procedures for dealing with illnesses, the professional qualifications of medical staff, and the relative availability of specialists inside and outside the prison. Then, the design of the plan and the skills of the faker matter. The characteristics of successful faking projects include picking illnesses with visible symptoms that can be simulated, a proper estimation of the faker's acting skills, and the lack of definite tests for a given illness, or at least the limited availability of any such tests.

Visible Symptoms

A master-faker can imitate numerous symptoms with simple tools and light self-injuries. Useful accessories include a razor, needle, piece of lead, salt, and blood. Even air and water may be used for sophisticated faking.

Blood may be added to one's stool or urine, or it can be swallowed. A master-faker Celebrak explains: "Look, guys, simple method. I take a needle . . . inject it in a vein and the blood is flowing, right? I got this needle in a hospital, I keep my eye on such stuff. I put about half a quart in a mug and added a bit of salt to keep it fresh. Inmates look at me fascinated. I ate a pound of bread, added three spoons of salt to the water, and drank it. And now I swallowed the blood from the mug. In a few minutes, I started vomiting. I vomited to a pot, to have an evidence [of bloody puke] for the guard. . . . Now, guys, hit the gate. The guard . . . calls a doctor . . . this must be a complete breakdown of your intestine. . ."[20]

Air can be pumped into various body parts in order to fake disorders: "I take a needle . . . mount a thin rubber pipe, inject the needle under skin on my head . . . and blow air [through the pipe] under my skull. My head gets cubical."[21] The stomach is the inmates' favorite body part: "I pump my abdomen with air. . . I simply swallow air and pump it to my stomach and guts . . . and my abdomen grows as if I were a woman expecting quadruplets . . . What is the best trick? They cannot X-ray a patient, since they cannot feed him the pulp that is necessary for X-rays."[22]

Various self-injuries may be used in order to produce the visible symptoms of a mental illness. A smart trick that could fool many doctors may work as follows: "I insert a thin needle into a heart chamber. You have to know where to put it. I know a guy who had thirteen needles in his heart. . . . And I pay attention not to put the needle entirely under the skin. I leave a tiny tip, so I could, when I press my skin, withdraw it back. I have a hairy chest, they will not notice. . . . 'You young idiot," the doctor tells me, 'you ruin your health this way.' Celebrak commented on the doctor's warning: "Certainly, there are sick people. But the majority of them are fakers, simulators, clowns. Eighty percent."[23] He also makes a more general point: "Psychiatrists claim that a normal guy will never cut himself. I disagree with them at this point . . . I went through all that myself and I had no psychiatric problems, I just wanted to reach my goals."[24] He was faking mental illness by apparently randomly hurting himself, while secretly taking care to minimize actual costs.

Acting

Acting is most important when one attempts to fake mental illness. Then, however, the "suspicion threshold" of the personnel is high, the period of observation very long, and the tricks to uncover fakers very sophisticated. The successful faker whose case is described next cleverly picked a disease with essentially all of the characteristics of a mental illness but without the associated difficulties.[25]

Frenchman was a high-class thief who specialized in burglarizing popular actresses, foreigners visiting communist Warsaw, and other potentially rewarding targets. He was charming, handsome, and spoke several languages. He told me and other cellmates that he had first noticed signs of Parkinson's Disease when he started to perform miserably in his finger-drills. Such drills are practiced routinely by incarcerated pickpockets in order to keep their professional skills intact. Frenchman had not contacted a doctor until he collapsed in the walkplace and injured his head. Then, after a brief physician's exam, he was transported to the Rakowiecka prison surgical cellblock.

Frenchman's stiff and gnarled limbs were shaking involuntarily during long bridge sessions and he made great effort to hold the cards. He moved slowly around the cell and while he tried to go for a walk from time to time, he was never able to make it. He fell a few times but always angrily rejected help. He never complained and used to tell the same joke to nurses and physicians: "You are wasting your time on me. Just give me a bottle of sedatives and everybody will be better off."

I was shifted to another cell at the time when Frenchman began his outside specialist consultations. Initially, he refused going to consultations since he was afraid of "looking at freedom" again. In fact, his first consultation in a Warsaw clinic made him so depressed that the doctors discreetly asked other inmates to keep their eye on him. They were afraid of an impulse-based suicide. Later, he cheered up and started talking about the professor who examined him and spent hours analyzing all of his words. Suddenly, it became clear to his cellmates and personnel that he had contracted outside of prison a disease he feared most: hope.

About three months after my release and less than four months after saying farewell to Frenchman, I met my cellmate while shopping at the Warsaw's Rozycki Bazaar flea market, a spot that attracted thieves and pickpockets. Frenchman was picking his way gracefully among the stands taking long, nimble steps. He glanced at me, blinked—and reciprocated my astonishment. Apparently, he was equally surprised to see his "cancer-stricken" jail-buddy free, alive, and well.

Frenchman, who was the only inmate classified by me on the spot as "having an incentive to fake and not faking," did a marvelous acting job. He made an impression on his cellmates and the personnel that he did not care about getting released, that he lost, and then regained, hope. He probably worked in cooperation with a freedom partner, at least one prison physician, and at least one specialist in a clinic. His illness was picked carefully. No single laboratory test can diagnose Parkinson's Disease! Thus, skillful acting combined with specialists' examinations were sufficient to provide credible documentation for his case.

Specialist Paperwork

The last case exemplifies the use of specialists' test results in faking. This successful faking project was based on the pancreatic cancer that Student had suffered seven years before he was incarcerated. Unfortunate patients with such a cancer have extremely low five-year survival rates of 2–4 percent due to a typically late diagnosis. Student's old history was used in order to produce documentation that the recovery had not been completed and that he suffered from repeated acute episodes of an inflammation of the pancreas, or pancreatitis, following incarceration. Pancreatitis is difficult to diagnose since its symptoms resemble the symptoms of other intestinal diseases. Untreated, it can lead to a patient's death. A possibility of the death of a sick inmate, supported with relevant documentation, makes the prison authorities and prosecutor more open to requests for release.

The idea of using the old cancer was voluntarily suggested to the Student's parents (who were physicians), by a Bialoleka prison nurse whom they contacted. The nurse's, and other doctors', willingness to help was clearly motivated both by professional solidarity and the political character of the case. The support for Solidarity among medical professionals in Poland of late communism was extremely strong. No bribes were offered or suggested at any stage of the faking.

The first step was to move the inmate from the Bialoleka general health room to the Rakowiecka hospital. The help of a trusted Rakowiecka surgical cellblock doctor was assured. Student's role was to produce visible symptoms such as a localized severe abdominal pain (eating a lot of fresh bread), diarrhea (salt water), and fever (catching colds). He complained about midback pain and general fatigue, lack of appetite, and signed up for all of the allowed physician visits.

At the surgical cellblock of the Rakowiecka prison, the case remained under the control of a physician contacted earlier by Student's parents with the help of the Bialoleka nurse. The doctor suggested a couple of trusted names in a freedom clinic. After a few weeks of "observation," the recommendation of follow-up specialized diagnosis tests was issued by the doctor. The patient was transported by armed prison guards to two outside consultations with the pancreas specialists. Various blood tests, along with ultrasonographic and tomographic exams, confirmed recurring episodes of pancreatitis that could lead to the patient's death. About three weeks later, Student was released. The faking saved an estimated two to seven months in prison.

Later, it turned out that the five months spent by Student in prison could have been probably shortened to a four-month period. The final diagnosis implying release was delayed by one month due to the "too good" performance of the patient. The recommendation to send the inmate from the Bialoleka prison for observation in the Rakowiecka hospital was not issued by the nurse's confidant doctor. During one of Student's frequent visits, another physician apparently became convinced by the unquestionable evidence of past disease and the consistency of the patients' complaints that a more detailed examination was necessary. However, the doctor recommended an observation at the Internal Medicine hospital cellblock of the Rakowiecka prison where no trusted physician could be identified. Then, it took about one month to transfer Student to the surgical cellblock and to advance to the outside-consultations stage.[26]

CHAPTER NINE

Exit

Release certificates almost always arrive in jail unexpectedly. Around midmorning a reptile may break the news and hand the disbelieving inmate the civilian clothes he once deposited in the storage cellblock. The certificate often states that the reasons behind the temporary arrest ceased to exist. This generic formula justifies the release to the same extent to which "the existence of important reasons" justified the arrest.

The first reaction of a shocked inmate is often an anxiety attack. All his business and trade plans are ruined. For me, the release notice initiated a brief eruption of "inmate happiness" which then gave way to a researcher's disappointment. My research was not yet finished. I had just received a new supply of tea, cigarettes, and a thick blank notebook and had become excited about building a research assistance network among my fellow-robbers, thieves, and felons. The arrangements for late night training were made with the cell elders, with plans to discuss grypsmen power hierarchies in various prisons. Two phlegmatic *faience-makers* had started chewing bread for my next order: five figurines of tiny handcuffed Donald Ducks and Mickey Mouses, their top-selling product. I was by far their best customer with an order valued at a full carton of cigarettes. For another two cartons, Chopin had agreed to fill my note-book with all the prison songs and tattoo motifs from his beloved scrapbook, and to throw in a set of tattoo equipment. I promised solemnly not to use them to set up a competing business. Suddenly, all of these arrangements looked terribly important. I considered asking the guards to let me stay for another weekend. But I had no money to bribe them.

After a while, the shock gives way to a sober planning for depar-ture. A crowd of vultures gathers slowly around the lucky inmate's bunk. They congratulate him cordially but their eyes wander rest-lessly over his stock of cigarettes, toothpaste, tea, and sugar. In a second, these goods lost most of their value in the owner's eyes. Maybe they can take advantage of his euphoria and get a bit free or cut a bargain? In fact, most of these once precious goods are traded cheaply for prison artifacts or just given away on exit.

The next step is hiding everything that one wants to smuggle out. First, I hid the most precious grypses and argot dictionary slips in my civilian underwear. The guards do not undertake deep per-sonal searches on exit. I put the prison shirt under a civilian one, squeezed the prison hat in the pocket, and fastened plates and spoon around my belly. If there is no search at all, all those souvenirs can be smuggled out. Then came requests from fellow grypsmen. Some of them rushed to write grypses and asked me to deliver them. I had a spotless reputation, so a few of them bet their safety on me.

Excited inmates waiting for release often fall into a talking trance. A harelipped Peasant was set free at the same time. He was locked up for stealing a cock, but—"I swear to my beloved freedom!"—it was only a hen—and he just wanted to caress it. "Those fucking communists, you know, they figured out my uncle was in Solidarity. I am a political prisoner, just as you are." Peasant got a release no-tice the day before but due to "objective difficulties" there was no-body to let him out. So he stayed an extra day. That happens often at Rakowiecka. Releases are usually on Fridays. It is convenient for the guards to open the storage only once or twice a week. Prosecu-tors cooperate and routinely sign all release certificates on Friday morning or Thursday afternoon. If one arrives earlier, it is usually delayed by a day or two. At least Peasant got an extra pint of milk for breakfast.

The familiar creaking at the gate announced the final farewell. The cell grypsmen formed a narrow passageway between the window and the gate, rolled towels, and put their boots on. Two long rows of inmates for whom our exit was only a brief break in the day's routine prepared for our last prison ritual, joking and exchanging trial punches. We stood by the window on the opposite side of the gate, leaning on the tigerbars and holding our *manchurs* firmly. This was not a baptism masquerade. This was our last grypsman rite of passage. The exit blows are real.

The reptile shouted our last names and the names of our fathers. Peasant entered the lane first. When he started running to the gate, the grypsmen started to hit his back with wet towels, kicked his bottom, swung their arms blindly in the hope of striking a good punch. "Farewell! Do not come back, Peasant. You are not welcome here, Student." They unloaded their frustration and disappointment that it was the other guy, not them. And, obviously, "hitting an exiting inmate hard improves one's odds for an early release." The bored guard stood in the gate looking on apathetically.

When Peasant started running, a sudden idea crossed my mind. I jumped ahead and followed him closely hoping that one cannot re-kick or re-punch so quickly. The reptile locked the gate. Peasant breathed heavily and wiped blood from his smashed harelip, happy that it was over. I felt sorry for him since I wasn't even touched. Five months ago I would have felt guilty. It was an unexpected strategic success in outsmarting my fellow grypsmen left behind the gate. I was sure that they noticed this smart run: "He left like a grypsman." Then they made mental notes to memorize one more trick. Just in case that long-awaited moment becomes a reality for them too.

Variants and Evolution of Grypsmen Subculture

LOCAL VARIANTS AND MODIFICATIONS

Conforming with the grypsing norms is, as with all human codes of behavior, erratic and sensitive to local interests and subjective interpretations. Moreover, the rigidity of code and argot varies across different communities. A local subculture may be restrictive, with strong enforcement of behavioral and language norms, or more relaxed, with less rigid conformity. The continuous incarceration of prisoners in their cells, as opposed to work outside the cell or prison, strengthens incentives for a strong local code. Cell size is another factor. Barns usually exhibit a rich subcultural tradition. The most violent and dramatic versions of the prison subculture tend to flourish in cells holding a large number of young inmates, whereas stability and the relaxation of harsh subcultural norms is more common in cells with higher proportions of recidivists. Thus, the list of most important variables affecting the strong adherence to norms would include the extent to which activities are concentrated in the cell, cell size, inmates' age, the relative power of the sucker group and possibly other castes, prison type, and the prison-specific level of administrative control. Other idiosyncratic factors can also be identified. For instance, the presence of political prisoners softens the harshest norms, especially those regulating relations with suckers and fags.

The various strengths of code are represented in the argot vocabulary. Under some circumstances, the code is automatically relaxed or strengthened. In addition to the regular code described earlier, a *relaxed code* allows for the relaxation of those norms that could be difficult to uphold and reduces the severity of sanctions. Usually under this type of code the education of a rookie comes to a halt. A loose code is assumed by default at prison hospitals and mental institutions. A loose code may also be implemented when the power of suckers and other groups is too serious to enforce separation or exploitation norms.

A *strict* or *rigid code*, or *red alert*, implies the strict enforcement of symbolic and argot norms. It is often maintained in cells or cell-blocks with the youngest offenders and can be imposed temporarily during the initiation period of America, as a means to rapidly socialize a rookie. It calls for the immediate sanctioning of the tiniest violations of argot and touching codes. The frequent instances of red alerts denote an environment where grypsmen have a strong grasp on power. Stepping is the most radical version of the strict code.

Under different modes of operation and configurations of relevant variables, inmate incentives to comply vary. When powerful interests collide with a norm, the interpretation of a norm may be molded to fit the interests. However, the strongest norms are associated with the least arbitrariness in interpretation and smallest variance in compliance. These norms include homosexual activity, touching the penis, maintaining clear social distance to fags, and unconditional ban on squealing. All "dirty physiology" norms are strictly enforced as well, but the sanctions for noncompliance are weaker. The social distance to suckers is much more susceptible to local power distribution and tends to decrease during the time that inmates spend together. In general, all symbolic norms are more likely to be re-interpreted, suspended, or even to disappear than the norms directly related to homosexual activity and sneaking. Their interpretation depends strongly on the context.

The same action may be interpreted differently under different circumstances. In Cell 6, Student shook a sucker's hand. He immediately received a harsh treatment from grypsmen, his secret grypsmen training was suspended, and he was effectively treated as a rookie on the path to becoming a sucker. In Cell 8, with the same status of rookie and potential sucker, Student offered a hand-shake to all the inmates on exit. Three out of four grypsmen accepted and only one, after hesitation, refused. In this cell, local norms were weaker and nobody had a strong interest in the strict enforcement of the symbolic norm. In Cell 6, Student's mistake followed a series of mishaps and violations and was used by the cell's fuss-maker in his own game. There was no point in offering a hand-shake on exit in this cell. It was evident that all eight grypsmen in this cell would refuse.

By 1985 a very interesting mechanism had been established that made the grypsmen less vulnerable to the attacks of outsiders. The local elders acquired the discretion to make case-by-case exemptions from certain norms should an important reason arise. While such interventions did not happen often, the decision-making mechanism was flexible enough to handle both minor and major adjustments.

During Student's time at the Rakowiecka hospital, the main case calling for special measures involved a dirty physiology norm. A sucker had surgery to create a fistula that redirected his bowels toward a substitute rectum in his belly. The rectum was extended with a disposable plastic bag. The sucker had no control over passing gas and, unfortunately, he tended to produce it during eating. An option of discoordinating the sucker and other inmates' meals was rejected as too inconvenient. After brief consultations, the cellblock elders allowed the cell grypsmen to eat without paying special attention to the random farts. Undoubtedly, it helped that the bag was sealed and the smell was trapped inside. Instead of announcing the fart, the sucker was required to announce when he was going to change his bag.[1]

The most profound relaxation of a secret code's norms took place at Rakowiecka three years before Student's incarceration. The arrival of Józef Korycki, called Robin Hood of Podlasie, caused a stormy debate involving all of the senior grypsmen at Rakowiecka and resulted in the temporary relaxation of the strongest norm of grypsing: penis touching. The life and agony of Robin Hood became one of Rakowiecka prison's greatest legends. His saga deserves a brief narrative.[2]

The Case of Robin Hood

Born in 1933, Robin Hood spent his entire life fighting communist officials, founding anticommunist organizations, and struggling for survival in communist prisons. His private war with communism started when, drafted to the communist army, he deserted, and kidnapped a Russian colonel on exit. When he was later caught, he was lucky to receive a short sentence since his desertion coincided with post-Stalinist thaw. When General Jaruzelski introduced Martial Law on December 13, 1981, he contemplated blowing up the nonstop Moscow-Berlin express, Mitropa, which carried the families of Soviet military personnel. He obtained dynamite and outlined the logistics of an attack. His friends from Solidarity, a movement founded on the orthodoxy of nonviolence, convinced him to abandon the idea of mass terrorism.

His last fight began in 1979, a month after his release from prison. Robin Hood modified the old idea implemented once by the famous outlaw of Sherwood Forest. This is how he made his nickname. He stole from the communist state and gave to poor farmers. His robbing model was based on a surprise visit to a village mayor known for his communist sympathies. A gentle giant, he would parade slowly through the village with a kalashnikov to the mayor's office and demand all the communist money. He was not interested in the official's personal belongings. Then he would distribute all of the proceeds among the needy farmers or tell them to buy a village tractor, he would play with local girls, eat, drink, and disappear. Before departing, he would order the village mayor to quit his job. All mayors complied with his orders. It was never necessary to pay a follow-up visit.

Robin Hood's actions were carefully planned and for a long time he managed to avoid trouble. He worked in Podlasie, a poor region of eastern Poland, where villages had no telephones and the roads resembled those of medieval England. The communist militia was always late. Farmers loved and supported him. They fed him and armed him with "just-in-case" weapons hidden after the Second World War ended with the communist takeover of Poland. Once, a delegation of farmers offered Robin Hood access to a working Soviet T-34 tank, carefully masked in a barn. It turned out upon inspection that the tank was in good shape, but the lack of ammunition made it useless.

After three successful years, the carelessness of one of Robin Hood's young companions tipped off the authorities. On May 14, 1982, the army raided his hideout with tanks, choppers, and hundreds of troops and militiamen. When the ring tightened, he decided not to go down with any killing on his conscience. Instead of fighting, he knelt down, put his kalashnikov on the ground, made the sign of the cross, and blew up his head with a Soviet nagan revolver. He woke up four days later at the Rakowiecka hospital. The left side of his body was paralyzed, his right arm was in plaster, and a bullet lay in his head. Miraculously, he survived. The militia boys wanted to kill him off but an army officer intervened.

The final chapter of his life saga unfolded in the prison hospital. A military prosecutor placed a retarded sucker in Robin Hood's solitary cell and promised him freedom for strangling the paralyzed bandit. However, the grypsmen quickly issued a protective warrant: Robin Hood's death would result in the sucker's execution. The sucker gave up and eventually started to help his cellmate. Both inmates were soon transferred to a regular hospital grypsmen cell.

The nurses used to ignore Robin Hood's requests for a bedpan. Since none of his hands were working, he defecated and urinated in bed. His linen and underwear were changed once a day. The code prevented his fellow grypsmen from helping him. Robin Hood knew the rules and did not complain. He smashed the plaster supporting his right arm and tried to regain his strength through working out. During these attempts, his paralyzed left arm slipped off the bed and got fractured. Hospital personnel did not intervene and the arm slowly knitted. Nobody ever heard him lamenting his fate.

Robin Hood's pitiful condition moved the grypsmen community and posed a tough dilemma for the local elders. No grypsman could doubt that Robin Hood was a fine robber, fierce anticommunist, loyal to the death, tougher than rock, that he was the incarnation of all grypsmen values. His record was transparent, confirmed by TV broadcasts and newspaper stories. He clearly deserved help. However, effective assistance would mean breaking one of the strongest norms and raised fundamental questions. Can a grypsman place a bedpan under another inmate's paralyzed body? Can a grypsman place a penis of his suffering pal in a bedpan? Can fundamental norms be relaxed for the comfort of the super-grypsman? Such problems were hotly debated in May and June 1982 at the Rakowiecka prison.

The grypsmen from Robin Hood's cell were unable to resolve the complex dilemma. Neither were the grypsmen at the hospital cellblock. Relaxing a fundamental norm without a proper consultation was risky and could result in the degradation of the entire cell or cellblock. Thus, the case went to the highest tribunal: the opinion of all prison elders. For days, grypses carried by corridormen and sent through diggers dealt exclusively with the case of Robin Hood's penis. The elders of Rakowiecka finally reached the unanimous verdict and endorsed a protocol for action.

The humiliation of a fine bandit, the prince of robbers, was decided to be a greater disgrace for the Rakowiecka grypsmen than violating the touching rule. Precise instructions were prepared for all those grypsmen who could be placed in Robin Hood's cell. If a fag was in the cell, the grypsmen were obliged to force him to service the man. If no fag was available, a designated grypsman was required to announce loudly to the personnel that Robin Hood needs to relieve himself. Then, after a few minutes of personnel inactivity, he was allowed to act himself. If the grypsmen in the cell were in good shape, they carried Robin Hood to feed the jaruzel. Otherwise, a bedpan could be delivered in place and Robin Hood's penis could be touched by another grypsman through toilet paper.

The grypsmen obeyed. For a couple of months, until Robin Hood's right arm recovered, grypsmen in his cell duly rotated as substitute nurses.

THE EVOLUTION OF GRYPSMEN SUBCULTURE

The changes of code over time are difficult to follow. Little analysis is available and some crucial phenomena are not described correctly in the literature. The best sources of data are prison dictionaries that offer valuable ethnographic material. Two such dictionaries by Michalski and Morawski (1971) and Stepniak (1993) provide an overall good description of the semi-secret argot. However, they fail to identify most secret rules and norms. Little games, the fundamental tests of a rookie's toughness and cleverness, are defined as games "that prisoners enjoy to play for fun"[3] or "customary methods of bullying new inmates."[4] Fag-making is implicitly identified with rape.[5] The argot itself is denoted with its old abandoned 1970s name "grypsera"; a "grypsman" is also called a "grypser," the term that since the 1970s denoted an inmate pretending to being a grypsman.[6] The signaling function of argot is not properly recognized. A number of the most typical blasphemies are described but the universal rationale behind them is missing.[7]

In spite of data scarcity, certain basic facts can be established. The first stage in the evolution of grypsmen subculture can be identified as the emergence of universal norms out of a narrower thieves' code. The second stage brought the pragmatization and further democratization of the formerly elitist subculture.

The relations of political prisoners carrying long sentences demonstrate that up to the end of 1956 no subculture resembling grypsing was widespread.[8] On the other hand, almost all of the components and accessories of grypsing were already present in the thief code. As related by a petty lifter, thieves played the role of grypsmen at the "thief prison" Gęsiówka in 1952. They had their own hierarchy and courts, applied simple little games to rookies and a version of fag-making, spun affairs, kept others off the table, observed some "dirty physiology" norms, prohibited blasphemies, and used extension rules. The thieves' slang, "kmina," was quite similar to the grypsmen argot. The lower categories of inmates included suckers, fags, cads, and others. On the other hand, the eligibility to the highest group was restricted to thieves. Thieves cooperated with the administration on many counts and had fewer touching taboos. For instance, every thief had a servant sucker who cleaned his dishes.[9] Grypsmen norms forbid suckers from dealing with their plates.

Prison literature from the early 1960s paints a different picture. The universal subculture of "charactermen," "gitmen," or "grypsers" was already in place.[10] The proportion of charactermen in prisons is estimated by one source at 14–38 percent[11] and, by two others, at 30–40 percent or 80–90 percent.[12] The argot vocabulary in the first edition of Michalski and Morawski's (1971) dictionary, published in 1967, closely resembles the 1985 version.

The expansion of the subculture seems to be related to the political thaw in the Soviet Bloc that followed Stalin's death in 1953 and Khrushchev's de-stalinization of 1956. Both the composition of incoming inmates and the prison constraints changed significantly. First, virtually all political and quasi-political prisoners were pardoned and since 1956 the proportion of such prisoners became insignificant. In addition, German Nazi prisoners were slowly dying out or getting released. Second, the prison rigors were relaxed and prisoners got more privileges, while the administration's resources remained virtually unchanged. For instance, implementing the rights of prisoners to a half-hour to an hour walk, introduced in the early 1950s, consumed substantial means: walking areas had to be built and a number of guards had to be delegated to the task of taking inmates to and from the walk. All of these changes increased the proportion of prison population of strict criminals and weakened the personnel's control over inmates.

The second deep transformation happened in the late 1960s and early 1970s and made the code more pragmatic and flexible. Instead of the strict observance of its letter, the power of interpreting its spirit and claiming exemptions and relaxations was transferred into the hands of the ruling elite. The changes made the code more robust to personnel manipulation and malicious sucker attacks. An especially dramatic change took place in the late 1960s when some prison personnel experimented with "de-grypsing" inmates. All newcomers were asked whether they were "grypsers." Since a grypser could not deny his caste membership, it was easy to identify

him. Then, he was beaten until he renounced his caste. Alternatively, he was thrown into a fiercely anti-grypsing cell. As a consequence, he was automatically degraded either by fellow grypsers or
suckers. Such a degradation was irreversible. The long-term reaction of the grypsmen community was a comprehensive change of
terminology: the word "grypser" was substituted by "grypsman"
and "grypser" acquired a different meaning, of an inmate pretending to be a grypsman. Thus, a grypsman was free to deny being
a grypser.[13] The argot assimilated the change immediately while
many researchers and personnel members mistakenly continued to
use the word "grypser" even thirty years later. The personnel's attempts at "de-grypsing" made the code even more flexible. In
1985, a grypsman was allowed to lie about his caste membership
under special circumstances, and a lift reversing degradation was an
important part of grypsmen customs.

The administration sometimes used its familiarity with grypsmen
verification procedures to degrade the most troublesome fuss-masters. A fake warning about a fuss-master in the Malbork prison coming originally from Poznan could be mailed from Poznan and
signed "The People." Then the fuss-master would get in trouble
with local grypsmen.[14] However, this method stopped working
when the grypsmen community learned about "de-grypsing" and
introduced double-checking and other backup procedures.

Another problem of the old rigid code, malicious sucker attacks,
was also partially solved. The condition that an offense against the
code must be "uncoerced and conscious" in order to lead to an
automatic sanction became increasingly prominent. The option of
restoring a grypsman's honor through self-injury was also introduced. The elders of various prisons nullified many norms that
would result in mass-scale fagotization. The lift of a forcefully fagotized grypsman became easier. The vertical social mobility among
castes became more dependent on the actual performance of inmates and on elders' interests rather than external factors.

The changes in the code affected various symbolic signs of power
and prestige. The importance of the criminal profession had diminished and high-caliber thieves lost their privileged position. In the

1960s, tattoos reflected grypsmen's social ranks. Fags and squealers were involuntarily marked with dots on their ears, cheeks, nose, or chin. Grypsmen wore dots tattooed on their fingers or eyelids and by their eyes. When a dot-marked grypsman became fagotized, a piece of brick was thrown under his feet. He had to use the brick to remove the misleading dots immediately. Military distinctions on shoulders represented the grypsman's prison tenure with ranks from private to marshal. The system soon became obsolete and faded away with other changes in the grypsman subculture. The shoulder ranks turned out to be poor carriers of status information. The distinctions were too easy to forge and hyperinflation followed. During the "de-grypsing" war, rank tattoos made it easier for the personnel to identify the grypsman elite. The final blow was provided by the prison administration when it applied the grypsman "brick degradation" method to their own highest-ranked officials. In some prisons, a new inmate officer was locked in a solitary cell with a brick and kept there until he rubbed the distinctions off his shoulders. With the demise of shoulder ranks, the systems of dot-marking fags, suckers, or squealers disappeared as well. All symbolic signs of power were overtaken by the importance of verifiable reputation and the familiarity with the subculture. The credible ability to apply brute force remained as important as it used to be.

Similar changes took place within the argot. Initially, a blasphemy thrown by a grypsman at another grypsman was as irremovable as his degradation. The strategic paradoxes created by this rule resulted in the gradual appearance of a variety of means of defense such as physical fighting and curse reversals. They were probably important to the introduction of stepping, the radical version of grypsman subculture, as well. The basic rules of stepping were supposedly worked out in the mid-1960s in Lodz, the second-largest Polish city, a few years after the subculture of grypsmen was formed in the dominant Warsaw prison environment.[15]

In the early years of self-injury and faking, inmates were often transferred to freedom hospital. Then, inmates self-injured themselves in order to relax security and hope for an opportunity to escape. The development of prison facilities for the treatment of main self-injuries virtually eliminated this motive.

While the evolution of the code and argot is somewhat a mystery, there is at least one naming convention whose evolution can be traced with good precision. The toilet bowl's name followed the changes in the communist leadership. Edward Gierek, who had ruled through the 1970s, still had a bunch of fans in 1985 who called the bowl *gier*. After the massive strikes led by Lech Walesa of the Gdansk Lenin Shipyard in 1980, Gierek was replaced in a typical communist coup by Stanislaw Kania. Kania's interim reign was too short to earn him a place in the argot hall of fame. General Jaruzelski, who took over the party leadership in 1981 and soon introduced the Martial Law, had been slowly winning on the naming battlefield as well. In 1985, despite a dozen alternative names, the "jaruzel" had become the favorite choice.

The fall of communism and the end of the millennium brought about some relaxation of the harshest punishments. Inmates were allowed to keep and drink tea and hold onto various personal belongings. All drillers could be turned off. Select cells received TV sets. Inmates were granted the right to occassional phone calls. However, it seems that the grypsmen subculture, code, and argot survived virtually unchanged.[16]

Prison Playground:

GAMES AND DECISIONS

A recurring theme of this book is that prison socializes inmates to hypercalculative behavior. In opposition to the freedom world, incorrect estimations of the consequences of everyday behavior result in extremely high costs. The paths of socialization are numerous. Working out a successful escape is impossible without careful planning, patience, and ingenuity. Responding to a sudden violent attack of another inmate requires making quick decisions on the spot. The very threat of a sudden attack motivates inmates to outline elaborate plans of action in advance. Self-injury, interrogation, trial, and many other situations involve careful calculation of the consequences of one's actions, relevant chances, and the actions of the others. A smart move can take years off one's sentence, secure better access to resources, prevent one from being raped or otherwise humiliated.

Inmates described in this book are involved in interactions of various kinds. They play games with rules known to everybody, face individual decision problems, test other unsuspecting fellow inmates, or form coalitions. In all their decisions, they take into account the specific physical and social constraints of everyday prison life. Many of the interactions can be represented with the help of game theory, a mathematical apparatus developed by mathematicians and economists in the mid-twentieth century to study rational behavior, as well as related approaches. This appendix informally describes main components of a sequential game and explains some of the unconventional notation used throughout the book.[1]

COMPONENTS OF A GAME: EXAMPLE OF THE PRISONER'S DILEMMA

Coincidentally, the best known game refers to a prison setup and is called the Prisoner's Dilemma (PD). The game was first analyzed in the 1950s by two RAND mathematicians, Dresher and Flood, and the illustrating story was devised by A. W. Tucker. The PD is used here to describe the main components of a sequential game and how we can represent interdependent decisions of players formally. Our version of the story runs as follows:

> Two presumed anticommunist activists, Dragon and Student, were arrested in Poland, then a communist country. There is enough evidence to convict them for the illegal possession of anticommunist Solidarity newsletters, which is a minor offense. However, there is not enough evidence to charge them with a more serious charge of publication and distribution of anticommunist books and newsletters. The prosecutor can indict them if at least one of them decides to testify. She places the suspects in separate isolated cells and tells Student how his testimony would affect his sentence. Student has two options: confess and "sell" his partner (C) or stay mum (M). Both prisoners care only about the length of their own sentences.
>
> If one of them confesses and the other stays mum, then the cooperating one would be released and the other would receive a harsh three-year sentence.
>
> If the prisoners both stay mum or both confess, they receive one year each for the minor offense or two years each, respectively.
>
> Next, the prosecutor tells the same story to Dragon.

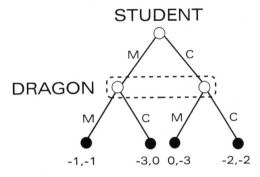

Figure A.1. The Prisoner's Dilemma.
Note: M—stay mum; *C*—confess.

The "dilemma" here is whether to confess or stay mum. Consider Student's decision problem. He cannot communicate with Dragon to coordinate their testimonies or otherwise affect his choice. Thus, Student evaluates the consequences of his own decisions assuming that they do not influence the decisions of Dragon. Two cases are possible:

Dragon stays mum: Then *C* leads to release and *M* brings one year.

Dragon confesses: Then *C* brings two years and *M* three years.

Since he cares only about his own sentence, Student is always better off when he confesses. Similarly, Dragon is always better off when he confesses. A strategy that, under all possible strategy combinations of the other players, is always better for player than any other his strategy, is called dominant. Now the problem: If the prisoners both confessed, they would receive a two-year sentence, while if they both stayed mum, they would only receive a one-year sentence! Thus, individually rational decisions—choosing a dominant strategy—lead to an outcome that makes both inmates worse off than if they had kept mum.

In figure A.1, PD is represented formally as a *sequential (extensive-form)* game.

In figure A.1, "Student" and "Dragon" denote the players. The white dots are the players' decision nodes, while the black dots mark terminal nodes or the end of the game. Two lines originating at the Student's decision node represent his two possible actions: confess or stay mum. Representing Dragon's options is slightly more complex. The graphical representation of a sequential game forces us to represent players' available actions sequentially even if they make simultaneous choices. The dotted line around Dragon's decision nodes takes care of this problem. It denotes the Dragon's "information set," that is, that he makes the decision simultaneously with Student or that he is not aware of Student's decision. Thus, the exact sequence of moves depicted in figure A.1 is in fact irrelevant and we could reverse it without altering the essential properties of our game. If the dotted line were not there, Dragon would know the Student's choice before making his own decision. Such a setup would define a slightly different game than the one described in our story. In such a case Student makes his decision first, then Dragon learns this decision and makes his own choice.

The last components of the game are the payoffs. The numbers below the terminal nodes represent the payoffs of both players in the same order in which the players make their moves. Thus, the first number indicates the payoff to Student while the second shows the payoff to Dragon. Since both players prefer less years in prison to more, the payoffs are the negatives of their sentences. In most games in this book, the payoffs denote only the ordering of preferences and not their intensity. The payoff associated with a player's least preferred outcome is the smallest number, say zero; the payoff at the second-least preferred outcome is the second-smallest number, say one, and so on. In other cases, when uncertainty is involved, the payoffs also represent players' attitudes toward risk with the assumption of a von Neumann-Morgenstern utility.

The PD game and its variants are used by social scientists to represent a variety of social, political, and economic phenomena, from arms races to electoral competition and environmental pollution. The "prison" story is just an illustration that makes it easier to understand the key properties of the game. The reader may ask at this point: So is the PD relevant to real investigation-interrogation situations? The answer to this question requires some elaboration. The PD in fact describes the "ideal" prosecutor's game, that is, the game that many prosecutors would like prisoners to believe they are playing. From a prosecutor's point of view, a PD is a wonderful mechanism for eliciting a confession. It is possible that designing a PD for suspects may be a natural starting point for many investigations. The author himself was placed in a PD-like situation. A squealer who was instructed by the prosecutor and probably worked as an undercover communist police agent was placed in the author's cell to entice him to cooperate. The squealer portrayed the author's situation in exactly the same way one would describe a PD.

However, the PD game does not represent all of the factors affecting the payoffs in actual investigations, even if the prosecutor sincerely believes that the numbers estimating sentences are accurate. The prisoners may estimate the expected sentences differently or they may be concerned with other factors as well. Thus, the PD can be used only as a starting point for a more comprehensive analysis. In his real-life dilemma, Student did not confess while Dragon—this prisoner's actual underground nickname—confessed. Both inmates were charged with the illegal publication of books considered as anticommunist and their legal situation was identical. However, Student's incarceration tenure ended after five months while Dragon had to wait a whole year. Thus, Student was ex post better off than Dragon, who had decided to cooperate with the prosecutor. Clearly, the ex post sentences both prisoners received are not consistent with those of the PD matrix since in a symmetric PD, a confessing inmate always gets a shorter sentence than the one who keeps mum.[2]

While this book is not concerned with investigation and interrogation games, it may be interesting to analyze selected factors that can transform the PD game as presented by the prosecutor into a different game.[3] Let's assume that the sentences in the game are indeed those of a PD.

First, prisoners may not necessarily be concerned exclusively with their own sentences. The factors disturbing the payoffs come from a variety of sources. Prisoners like Bonnie and Clyde may care about their partners. High-profile dissidents and other political prisoners may care about their reputation or reject cooperation with a regime on moral grounds. Confessing and "selling" partners may also be severely punished by the mafia or by the prisoners themselves, as in the case of grypsmen.

Second, the game takes place over a longer period of time, involves many interactions, and the menu of relevant options is richer than the binary "confess-mum" would suggest. The prosecutor cannot change some aspects of the law. If one inmate confesses, then the other inmate may always retaliate with his own confession. An interrogation confession may later be withdrawn. The inmates may exercise pressure on the prosecutor with self-injuries. Also, the isolation of suspects may be an unrealistic assumption when they have, unlike their communist counterparts, the right to contact a lawyer before the interrogation begins. Even without the intermediating lawyer, inmates may work out other communication channels and mechanisms for coordinating testimonies.

Whether a particular game adequately represents player interactions depends on the proper recognition of all those factors affecting the game's setup: relevant players, the actions available to them, their information and payoffs. A good model should be well-grounded in the empirical world it seeks to represent and built upon sound intuitions.

NON-STANDARD REPRESENTATIONS OF GAMES

This section outlines how the various nonstandard "games of deception" in this book can be converted into more standard games of incomplete information. Needless to say, this section is not intended to develop a fully formalized family of games with corresponding solution concepts. Its aim is to convince a potentially skeptical game theorist that certain intuitions represented in games of deception can receive a plausible formal representation.

The rationale for adopting various nonstandard representations is simple. Full-scale games of incomplete information that model complex interactions, or other formal models representing the lack of common knowledge among players, would be difficult to understand without the use of more advanced mathematics. A nonspecial-

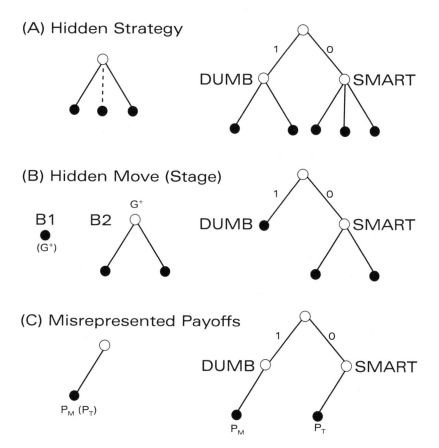

Figure A.2. Games of deception.

Note: Schematic ideas of how deception games (pictures on the left-hand side) can be converted into corresponding games of incomplete information with relevant probabilities of being 'smart' or 'dumb' (pictures on the right-hand side): (A) Player is unaware of his own strategy. The dotted line denotes the "hidden" strategy; (B) Player at the node depicted in B1 is unaware that his opponent has an extra move depicted in B2. The "hidden" subgame is shown in parentheses in B1; (C) Player misrepresents his or his opponent's payoffs. The "true" payoff is shown in parentheses.

ist reader would be quickly bored with such models and distracted from the more important and substantive messages of the book. Thus, in many cases a potentially more general model was divided into smaller pieces or its presentation was simplified with a convention that carried the intuition in a concise way.

The following conventions were applied in the games that can be called the "games of deception":

1. Player is not aware of the existence of a strategy (the "hidden" strategy is represented by a dotted line, as in figures 1.1 and 3.5);
2. Player does not know that the game does not end (the payoffs are followed by parentheses with a symbol denoting that part of the game which the player is unaware of, as in figure 3.6);
3. Player incorrectly estimates payoffs (the incorrect payoffs are followed by parentheses with the correct payoffs, as in figures 1.1 and 3.2).

All three representations described above could be substituted with standard games of incomplete information that would represent very closely related decision problems. Such representations would allow for the application of solution concepts such as Bayesian or perfect Bayesian equilibrium that are standard for games of incomplete information. The price would be paid in the increased complexity of the models (see figure A.2).

The idea behind converting a game of deception into a closely related standard game of incomplete information is simple. Informally, there are two possible types of players: an informed (smart) one and an uninformed (dumb or deceived) one. Nature chooses the type of player according to some probability distribution; every such distribution denotes a specific game. The part of the game tree corresponding to the uninformed player in a game of deception is represented by a relevant game of incomplete information with the probability of choosing the uninformed player being equal to 1. Conversely, when a player is informed, then in the corresponding game of incomplete information the probability of choosing the informed player is equal to 1.

Problems described here are related to relaxing the assumption of common knowledge in games. An interested reader may consult Fudenberg and Tirole (1991) for references.

Essential Argot

Words are presented in the following format: English name [Polish original name] *alternate names*—definition. If no Polish term is given, then it is identical with its English equivalent. "Am. counterpart" means that an American argot term was used to represent a corresponding Polish argot term. Some of the synonyms are not translated from Polish. Only the most frequently used synonymical name appears on the list. Little games and self-injury techniques that are described separately in the text are usually omitted.

affair [afera, zadyma] — case involving evidence gathering and debating that follows a supposed violation of a major norm by a grypsmen

America [Ameryka] — a rookie's trial period before he joins the grypsmen or a lower caste

aproposman [apropak, apropaka] — inmate using frequently difficult and elitist words such as "apropos"

back to you [ze zwrotem] — expression reversing a blasphemy

bajera — 1. Prison university. 2. Argot. 3. Long story-telling session with czajura. 4. The ability to talk in an engaging manner.

baptism [chrzest] — test applied to candidates for grypsmen in barns

barn [stodoła] — large cell hosting 40–50 inmates

blinda — a sheet of thick translucent glass with an embedded metal net blocking one's sight from a window and placed outside of the cell

boil [kipisz] — search of a cell or inmate

cat [kot, świr] — inmate who is mentally ill or simulating mental defects

chief [wódz], commandant [dowódca], mister block-leader [pan oddziałowy] — prison guard's name when addressed by inmates. See also: reptile.

corridorman [korytarzowy], kajfus, kalifaktor — inmate distributing food or other goods among cells

cottage cheese [twaróg] — white discharge left on the penis after nightly pollution

cube [kostka] — inmates' clothes folded for the night and placed outside the cell by the gate

curfew, night alert — time after going to bed and before the wake-up bell, when eating is prohibited and masturbation is allowed by grypsmens' norms

czajura — tea infusion prepared illegally by inmates

digger [przebitka] — horizontal or, less frequently, vertical hole in a cell's wall that inmates use to communicate and trade with other cells

dill [koperek] — female pubic hair or underwear with vaginal secretions

drill, pneumatic drill [betoniara] — speaker fixed over the cell's gate, often centrally turned on and off, active 6:00–11:00 A.M. and 3:00–9:00 P.M.

elder [starszyzna] — a member of the core ruling cell elite among grypsmen

ensign [chorągiewa], grypser — a nongrypsman pretending to be a grypsman in a new cell or prison

fag [cwel, Am. counterpart], pipe [rura] — a member of the lowest caste of inmates, who provides or provided in the past sexual services to other inmates, or who was raped or otherwise sexually humiliated. See also: grypsman, sucker *fag-making [przecwelanie]* — test applied to a rookie in which he is tempted to sexually please a grypsman in exchange for a promise of protection

fagotization [przecwelenie] — 1. Degradation of an inmate to sucker or fag status. 2. Changing the status of an object from pure or dirty to untouchable. 3. Breaking down: The lightbulb got fagotized

feeder [karmnik, karmik] — a small valve in the gate used for food and other goods distribution

for fun [w kit] — expression nullifying a blasphemy

fuss-maker [zadymiarz] — 1. Inmate skillfully spinning affairs in order to profit from such activity. 2. Inmate presently spinning an affair

fuss-master [mąciciel, kierownik zadymy] — chief grypsman at the level of cell, cellblock, or prison

gate [klapa] — metal cell doors

go-on [nawiń] — expression coordinating window-shouting used to indicate that a person is ready to receive next message (similar to "roger")

gryps — secret message smuggled from prison or circulated within prison

grypser — 1. In late 1960s and early 1970s a name denoting grypsman. 2. From 1970s on: *ensign*, a nongrypsman who pretends to be a grypsman in a new cell or prison

grypsman [grypsujący], man [człowiek] — a member of the most powerful caste of inmates in Polish prison. See also: sucker, fag.

hardbed [twarde, twarde łoże] — 1. Solitary confinement. 2. Block of concrete imitating a bed in solitary confinement cells.

hay [sianko], materek — mattress used by bedless inmates

herod — very old inmate, older than zgred

jaruzel, throne [tron], pot [dzban], [bardacha, klop, gier] — toilet bowl

jumper [skakaniec] — hyperactive inmate who unconvincingly brags about his adventures and connections, etc.

lift [podniesienie] — infrequent ceremony in which a sucker is upgraded to a grypsman *manchur [mandżur]* — inmates' belongings packed for a shift in a sack made of a blanket

muster [apel, raport] — morning and evening examination of a cell by a guard

newbie [nowy, Am. counterpart] — a former inmate re-entering prison or an inmate transferred from another prison unit

offense [wychyła] — violation of norms of grypsing, sometimes leading to the degradation to sucker or fag status

pneumatic drill — see drill

principles [zasady] — five general principles of grypsing: solidarity, noncooperation, help, honor, hygiene

rehab [wychowek] — prison counselor taking care of inmates' rehabilitation

report [raport] — description of a violation of an administrative rule by one or more inmates, prepared by a guard or rehab and leading to punishment

reptile [gad], key [klucz], red spider [czerwony pająk], bitch [kurwa] — prison guard's name used among inmates. See also: chief

rocket [rakieta] — a parcel from family with food or clothes

rookie [świeżak, Am. counterpart], American [Amerykan] — a new inmate, first time in prison

scepter [berło] — toilet brush. When touched with a scepter, a grypsman may become degraded to a sucker

silter [zamuł, zamuleniec] — a depressed inmate

spinning an affair [wykręcić aferę] — claiming a violation of major grypsing norm by another grypsmen and gathering relevant evidence

squealer [konfident, kapuś, Am. counterpart] — inmate squealing on cellmates or his partners in crime

stepping [kopytkowanie] — a radical version of grypsing with more comprehensive argot rules and a stricter norm enforcement

sucker [frajer, Am. counterpart], nongrypsman [niegrypsujący] — a member of the intermediate caste of inmates. See also: grypsman, fag

swap [podmianka] — illegal temporary change of cells by inmates, conducted after a joint walk by a few cells *tigerbars [tygrysówa]* — thick iron bars protecting the cell window from the inside or outside

Titanic [Batory, Am. counterpart] — mobile container transporting coffee and food for distribution among cells

walkplace [spacerniak, spacernik] — a 50–100 m² fenced yard where inmates are taken by guards for a 20–50 minute walk

youngster [małolat] — inmate less than 21 years old

zgred — old inmate

Notes

INTRODUCTION

1. The subculture of Polish prisons survived the fall of communism and subsequent events with surprisingly few changes. A more elaborate comment on the relevance of the subculture painted in the book is included in the "Postscriptum."
2. Moczydlowski 1992.
3. Kaminski 1988.
4. For instance, Bukovsky (1979: 26) writes, "No matter how many prison memoirs [external spectators] might have read, they will never be able to understand [the importance of] trivial and minor details [of prison life]."
5. In the book, I use a popular phrase "freedom x," where "x" may be world, woman, hospital, etc., instead of "free x." The meaning of "freedom x" in argot is close to "x coming from the other world, called freedom."
6. Solzhenitsyn 1979: 3–5.
7. The term *grypsman*, denoting an inmate from the highest caste, is derived from *gryps*, denoting a secret message delivered within or smuggled outside of prison. Grypsmen communicate frequently with grypses and maintain efficient delivery channels. Other inmates smuggle grypses occasionally.
8. Sykes 1999: 135.

CHAPTER ONE
ENTRY

1. A prisoner is often referred to hereafter as an *inmate*; first-timers are called *rookies*; inmates transferred from another unit or re-entering as recidivists are called *newbies*; the ruling inmate elite are called *elders*.

CHAPTER TWO
THE CONSTRAINTS OF PRISON LIFE

Parts of this chapter were published in Kaminski and Gibbons 1994.
1. Sykes and Messinger 1960.
2. Sykes 1999.
3. Mums 1985a. Communist estimates for different audiences varied greatly. For instance, the officially released number of all prisoners in 1980 was 105,509. The secret note distributed among penitentiary judges increased this number to over 138,000. The statistics were manipulated by implicitly using different definitions of prisoners in different calculations. Often, inmates from jails and other types of prison were excluded from the officially published data (Mums 1985a).
4. Interestingly, in American prisons, such as Alcatraz, the main halls in cell-blocks are often called *Broadway*.

5. Mums 1985b.
6. Goffman 1961.
7. Conversely, in American prisons social mobility among roles is not limited since the roles do not represent formal labels assigned by the strongest group but rather "alternative modes of adjustment to problems of prison life" (Garabedian 1963: 143).
8. Moczydlowski 1992.
9. Gibbons 1992b: 501–20.

CHAPTER THREE
BECOMING A GRYPSMAN

This chapter is a modified version of Kaminski 2003.
1. Goffman (1961: xiii) defines a total institution as a "place of residence and work when a large number of like-situated individuals, cut off from the wider society for an appreciable period of time, together lead an enclosed, formally administered round of life." Prisons and jails, P.O.W. and concentration camps, mental hospitals, leprosaria, boarding schools, orphanages, large plantations, military bases, submarines and ships, fraternities, or monasteries share many characteristics of a generic total institution.
2. Sykes 1999: 86.
3. Clemmer (1940: 299) defines "prisonization" as "the taking on, in greater or lesser degree, of the folkways, mores, customs, and general culture of the penitentiary." He notes that strong local subculture speeds up prisonization.
4. Scenarios of typical prison movies are constructed around unusual displays of toughness and/or cleverness. In *The Bridge over the River Kwai*, the character played by Alec Guinness, after passing a severe test of *toughness*, confuses everybody with a behavior attributable to a converted *weakling*. All "incredible-escape" movies, such as *The Shawshank Redemption* and *The Great Escape*, employ the cleverness motif. *Cool Hand Luke* explores the combination of both factors. A *tough* character played by Paul Newman cleverly persuades the guards that he is *broken* in order to organize an escape. "Cleverness" does not denote "wisdom" or "conversational skills" but rather the gift of a quick and witty reaction to an unusual situation. Miller (1958) identifies "autonomy," in addition to toughness and smartness, as a third core value among delinquent adolescents and prisoners who accept the norms of the *thieves* group in American prisons.
5. See Geresz 1986: 26, and Kaminski and Gibbons 1994: 112.
6. This is a precise reconstruction of a test that I was subjected to in Cell 6 and an offer I received from my cellmate Maniek. A similar scenario was then described during secret grypsmen training. Two rapes that happened in cells adjacent to my cell were executed according to a similar scenario. Inmate relations referring implicitly or explicitly to a nonviolent character of prison rapes include Geresz (1986: 26), Trebicki (1988: 17), and Wojciechowski (1981: 139–40).
7. I was subjected to baptism in Cell 13. The typical character of this scenario was then confirmed in subsequent conversations with old cell dwellers.

8. I was subjected to most of the little games described in this section in Cell 6. Other little games were reconstructed during tea-chats and conversations in Cells 7–13. Selected little games are described in Geresz 1986, Gluza 1987, Michalski and Morawski 1971, Stepniak 1993, Stwora 1993, Trebicki 1988, and others.

9. See for instance Bukovsky 1979: 306, Herling 1974: 18.

10. Stwora 1993.

11. Hidden tests were reconstructed on the basis of my experience in Cell 6 and other inmates' tests in Cells 8 and 13.

12. I was subjected to regular secret training in Cells 6, 8, and 13 and to its informal version in Cells 7, 9, 10, 12.

13. The word "bajera" has numerous meanings in addition to "prison university": it is often used to denote the prison language itself, telling long stories, or the ability to talk in an engaging manner.

CHAPTER FOUR
PRISON CODE OF BEHAVIOR

This chapter is based almost exclusively on the author's prison notes and synthesizes the material collected in Cells 6–13. The norms of the grypsmen secret code are described for the first time in such detail.

1. Principles represent grypsmen's solutions to what Sykes calls the "pains of imprisonment" in American prisons.

2. Reconstructed from one of Student's cross-examinations in Cell 13.

3. Window-shouting as a means of communication is described in chapter 6.

4. Niesiolowski 1989: 98–9.

5. A stylized typical minor affair.

6. Case recorded in Cell 13.

7. Case recorded in Cell 13.

CHAPTER FIVE
ARGOT

1. Most of the words and selected grammar rules, especially less secret ones, were described earlier, especially in the dictionaries of Michalski and Morawski (1971) and Stepniak (1993). The primary contribution of the present chapter is the comprehensive reconstruction of secret argot grammar.

2. Recorded in Cell 8.

3. Sykes 1999.

4. See, e.g., Clemmer 1940, Sykes 1999, Schrag 1961, Heffernan 1972, Bowker 1977, Thomas and Petersen 1977. The catalog of American argot roles reviewed below is from Sykes 1999.

5. Garabedian 1963: 144.

6. Sykes 1999: 106.

7. Prince in Cell 9 and Cat in Cell 12.

8. The language duel was recorded live in Cell 7.

9. Student was asked this very popular question and the next question in Cell 6.

10. See Geresz 1996.
11. The next four questions were recorded in Cell 7.
12. All jokes were recorded in Cells 7 and 8.

CHAPTER SIX
EVERYDAY LIFE

1. The entry technique was described to me by Prince in Cell 9.
2. Moczydlowski 1992: 52–3.
3. A stylized typical conversation.
4. See Gluza 1987: 19.
5. Recorded in Cell 6.
6. Niesiolowski 1989: 116.
7. Copied from a singer's scrapbook in Cell 13. A slightly modified version of this popular song appears in Trebicki 1988.
8. Stwora 1993: 26.
9. Trebicki 1988: 74.
10. Notes describing Skull's tattoos were taken in Cell 7 after tea-chats. The meaning of various pictures was explained by their owner.
11. The trick of Skull, who collected toll over three weeks that I spent in Cell 7 from three inmates, including me.
12. The rationale behind making tea illegal is unclear. Most likely, since preparing tea involves using electricity and boiling water, allowing these activities could offer inmates easier opportunity for self-injury.
13. A generic procedure applied on a daily basis in Cells 4, 6–10, 12–13.
14. Niesiolowski 1989: 181.
15. From a tea-chat in Cell 6.
16. From tea-chats in Cells 6, 7, and 13.
17. Gambetta 2003 considers a similar model. He stresses the type-revealing function of prison violence.
18. Recorded in Cell 8.
19. Boxer in Cell 7.

CHAPTER SEVEN
SEX, FLIRTATION, LOVE

1. Student was repeatedly asked this popular and intentionally embarrassing question by Zgredzio and Spaniard in Cell 6.
2. Trebicki 1988: 110.
3. As discussed among grypsmen in Cell 6. See also Trebicki 1988: 27.
4. From a typical nightly story by Spaniard in Cell 6 and other tea-chats.
5. Recorded from nightly inmate behavior in small regular Cells 6 and 8. See also Wojciechowski (1981: 138–40) for a similar description.
6. Trebicki 1988: 167.
7. A number of swaps took place in Cells 6 and 13.
8. Reconstructed from conversations in Cell 13 referring to a recent incident.
9. Recorded during a tea-chat in Cell 13.
10. Trebicki 1988: 123–4.

11. Max in Cell 6.
12. Stwora 1993: 54.
13. Recorded live by Niesiolowski 1989: 116–117.
14. Trebicki 1988: 234.
15. Trebicki 1988: 235.
16. Recorded in Cell 13.
17. Recorded in Cell 13; also recorded by Moczydlowski 1992: 24–5.

CHAPTER EIGHT
STRATEGIC AILMENT

1. Various political prisoners-turned-authors not only recorded numerous techniques of faking illness and self-injury but also engaged in strategic ailment themselves (see Bukovsky 1979: 262, 317–18, 252, 393–5; Herling 1974: 18, 102). Wantchekon combined faking and self-injury in order to get transferred to a prison hospital and eventually to escape (personal communication). I applied light self-injury and physician-supported faking in order to get an early release.

2. Other kinds of strategic ailment are less frequent. An example is the case of Robin Hood, described in detail in Postscriptum. Partially paralyzed, Robin Hood waited for surgery that would remove a bullet from his head. He strategically refused surgery since he believed that (i) the prison surgeons were not well qualified and there was a high probability that he would die; (ii) even if he recovered, a trial would immediately follow and he would be sentenced to death. (Robin Hood described his beliefs to me in Cell 10.) Cases in the "other" category seem to be rare and mainly limited to the attrition game of a truly sick inmate who has to accept or deny a certain medical procedure. I recorded two more cases of strategic surgery denial.

3. Mums 1986a: 76.

4. Stwora 1993: 109.

5. Michalski and Morawski 1971: 59.

6. Alaska 1986: 79–81. A comprehensive set of surveys was conducted in 1978–79 in sixteen prisons. Half of the sample consisted of self-injurers. An exact sample size was not reported.

7. Virtually all techniques listed in the catalogue were observed or discussed by Student in Cells 7, 9, 10, 11, 12, 13. All descriptions except for *seesaw* are based on multiple first-hand accounts. Seesaw was described in Cell 11 by a junkie Tomek, who was rescued by guards and was later released with a suspended sentence. Second-hand relations were consistent with Tomek's first-hand account. Techniques such as cutting, dusting, hunger strike, injection, nailing, scalding, and swallow were gradually identified by physicians and personnel in the late 1960s and early 1970s.

8. Mums 1986a: 76–7.

9. Stwora 1993.

10. The technique was demonstrated to Student in Cell 12 by Cat, an experienced swallower, during an hour-long session.

11. The distinction between signaling and pragmatic self-injuries was clarified in an online exchange with Diego Gambetta.

12. p may also be interpreted as the probability assigned by the elders that a given grypsman is loyal or disloyal.

13.   In reference to the game "Cry of Desperation," the term equilibrium denotes perfect Bayesian Nash equilibrium in pure strategies.

14.   The critical level for the "Cry of Desperation" game is $p^* = 0.5$. The significance of this particular number results from the simplifying assumption about the elders' preferences. In a slightly more general model, p^* would be a function of the utilities associated with degrading loyal and disloyal types versus maintaining their status quo.

15.   Trebicki 1988: 103.

16.   Trebicki 1988.

17.   Recorded in Cell 10. The method used in this case was a swallow: Two inmates from Bialoleka and Rakowiecka prisons were transported to the Rakowiecka prison surgery cellblock.

18.   Hepatitis A can be contracted only through the digestive system while hepatitis B may be contracted only through blood, e.g., injection. It was not possible to check what kind of hepatitis the fuss-master had access to. Note that in 1985, inmates were unfamiliar with HIV. I was offered access to hepatitis as well, but did not take it given my expected shorter sentence. If the expected shortening of the sentence were of an order of magnitude of the fuss-master's 3.5 years, then such an option would certainly have been considered.

19.   Case recorded in Cells 9–12, described in Kaminski 1993: 134–5.

20.   Stwora 1993: 75.

21.   Stwora 1993: 117.

22.   Stwora 1993: 105.

23.   Stwora 1993: 118.

24.   Stwora 1993: 107.

25.   Case recorded in Cell 12.

26.   Reconstructed from the notes of Mikolaj Kaminski (1985).

POSTSCRIPTUM
VARIANTS AND EVOLUTION OF GRYPSMEN SUBCULTURE

1.   Recorded in Cell 12.

2.   The Robin Hood's case is reconstructed from my numerous conversations with Robin Hood in Cell 10, newspaper clips, and the multiple accounts of other inmates.

3.   Stepniak 1993: 157.

4.   Michalski and Morawski 1971: 69.

5.   Michalski and Morawski 1971: 22.

6.   Stepniak 1993: 172–3.

7.   Michalski and Morawski 1971: 16–7; Stepniak 1993: 45.

8.   See, e.g., Chmielewski 1991; Slaski 1992.

9.   Wojciechowski 1981. There are many similarities between the codes of Polish thieves and grypsmen, and the code of Soviet *vory-v-zakone* (*thieves-with-a-code-of-honor*). Similarities include entry rituals, various little games and tricks,

cases of similar or identical argot words, behavior norms, or conflict arbitration institutions (see Varese 2001: 145, 166).

10. Michalski and Morawski 1971; Stwora 1993; Moczydlowski 1991.

11. Michalski and Morawski 1971.

12. Moczydlowski 1992: 116.

13. Moczydlowski 1992: 114–16.

14. Moczydlowski 1992: 117.

15. Stepniak 1993: 174.

16. Paradoxically, the fall of communism ended the flow of detailed accounts from prison. The reason is simple: almost all interesting accounts were by political prisoners thrown into cells with criminal ones. The incarceration of such inmates ended with the demise of communism. I did find a couple of short accounts by former criminal prisoners who describe or mention various components of prison subculture. Among over thirty argot words that they used, all of them were known in the 1980s. The key terms of "grypsman," "sucker," "reptile," "rehab," and "principles" were mentioned. One of the authors, a sucker, called "grypsmen" by the incorrect name of "grypsers." Grypsmen often misled rookie suckers with this name in order to keep them uninformed, at least for some period of time. Grypsmen still adhered to the same or a similar set of "principles" and "dirty physiology" rules, the norm that a newbie must not be raped without his consent was mentioned, a grypsman who broke norms was degraded to the status of sucker, newbies went through a period of "America," etc. (Luporum 2000; Anonymous 2001; Wieclawski 2002).

APPENDIX
PRISON PLAYGROUND

1. The Appendix is obviously not a substitute for an introductory course in game theory. Its objective is only to explain basic conventions of game theory as well as some nonstandard notation adopted in this book. A curious reader will be delighted to learn that many good introductory game theory textbooks, written mainly by economists, are available. Dixit and Nalebuff (1991) is perhaps the least formal and most accessible one. Among more advanced textbooks intended for an undergraduate student with some grasp of calculus and taste for mathematical puzzles, Gibbons (1992b) and Ordeshook (1986) provide more formal introductions to applications to economics and political science, respectively. Luce and Raiffa (1957) and Brams (1975) are slightly dated now but highly rewarding readings. I wholeheartedly recommend to an interested reader to enroll in an undergraduate course of game theory for economists or political scientists. Such courses are routinely taught at all research universities. Expect big intellectual rewards.

2. In Student's case, the prosecutor was unable to enforce his threat of a long sentence given the political thaw that resulted from Gorbachev's *perestroika*. The periodic amnesties for political prisoners as well as a successful faking of illness by Student also undermined his ability to enforce the threat. Student's preferences were typical of many "Solidarity" activists who also refused to testify regardless of

the associated sentence. Dragon's preferences—according to his own post-release account—represented his desire to minimize his incarceration time.

3.   One of the few game-theoretic analyses of interrogation and a corresponding "game of torture" is provided by Wantchekon and Healy (1999). Leonard Wantchekon, a game theorist and political activist in Benin, had escaped from prison after two years of incarceration thanks to a successful faking and a light self-injury.

References

Alaska. 1986. Samookaleczenia. (Self-injuries.) *Praworzadnosc* III (12/13): 78–82.

Anonymous. 2001. *Dzwieki (Sounds)*. Available from www.republika.pl/ zk_stargardszcz.

Bowker, Lee H. 1977. *Prisoner Subcultures.* Lexington, MA: Lexington Books.

Brams, Steven. 1975. *Game Theory and Politics.* New York: Free Press.

Bukovsky, Vladimir. 1979. *To Build a Castle—My Life as a Dissenter.* New York: Viking Press.

Chmielewski, Franciszek. 1991. *'Kwadrans' na Rakowieckiej, 1948–1956.* ('Fifteen minutes' at Rakowiecka, 1948–1956.) Warszawa: Bellona.

Clemmer, Donald. 1940. *The Prison Community.* Boston: Christopher.

Cressey, Donald R., and Witold Krassowski. 1957/58. Inmate Organization and Anomie in American Prisons and Soviet Labor Camps. *Social Problems* 5 (Winter): 217–30.

Dixit, Avinash, and Barry Nalebuff. 1991. *Thinking Strategically. The Competitive Edge in Business, Politics and Everyday Life*: New York: W. W. Norton.

Fisher, S. 1965. Informal Organization in a Correctional Setting. *Social Problems* 13 (Fall): 214–222.

Fudenberg, Drew, and Jean Tirole. 1991. *Game Theory*: Cambridge, MA: MIT Press.

Gambetta, Diego. 2003. Violence and Information in Prison. In *Crimes and Signs: Essays on Underworld Communication.* Unpublished manuscript.

Garabedian, Peter, G. 1963. Social Roles and Processes of Socialization in the Prison Community. *Social Problems* 11: 139–52.

Geresz, Jerzy. 1986. Relacja. (Relation.) In *Polityczni. Wiezniowie polityczni w Polsce lat 1981–1986*, edited by A. Szanski. Warszawa: Przedswit.

Gibbons, Don, C. 1992a. *Society, Crime and Criminal Behavior.* 6th ed. Englewood Cliffs, NJ: Prentice Hall.

Gibbons, Robert. 1992b. *Game Theory for Applied Economists.* Princeton, N.J.: Princeton University Press.

Gluza, Zbigniew. 1987. *Epizod. Dziennik zamkniecia.* (Episode. The Diary of Incarceration.) Warszawa: Przedswit.

Goffman. 1961. On the Characteristics of Total Institutions: The Inmate World. In *The Prison*, edited by D. R. Cressey. New York: Holt, Reinehart & Winston.

Heffernan, Esther. 1972. *Making It in Prison: The Square, the Cool, and the Life.* New York: Wiley.

Herling, Gustav. 1974. *A World Apart.* Westport, CT: Greenwood Press.

Kaminski, Marek, M. 1988. Badacz i uczestnik. Procesy poznawania wiezienia. (Researcher and Participant. The processes of researching prison.) Unpublished Masters thesis, Instytut Socjologii, Uniwersytet Warszawski, Warszawa.

Kaminski, Marek M. 1993. Racjonalny wiezien. Subkultura grypsowania aresztow sledczych w Bialolece i na Rakowieckiej w 1985 roku. (Rational Prisoner. The Subculture of Grypsmen in Bialoleka and Rakowiecka Jails.) *Studia Socjologiczne* (3–4): 115–38.

Kaminski, Marek M. and Don C. Gibbons. 1994. Prison Subculture in Poland. *Crime and Delinquency* 40 (1): 105–19.

Kaminski, Marek, M. 2003. Games Prisoners Play. Allocation of Social Roles in a Total Institution. *Rationality and Society* 15(2): 188–218.

Kaminski, Mikolaj, ed. 1985. *Z tej strony bramy (On this side of the gate.)* Unpublished manuscript in the author's collection.

Luce, R. D., and H. Raiffa. 1957. *Games and Decisions.* New York: Wiley.

Luporum, Lupuss. 2000 *Kryminal—mity i fakty. (Prison—myths and facts.)* Available online at www.nara.qp.pl.

Michalski, Henryk, and Jacek Morawski. 1971. *Slownik gwary wieziennej.* (The Dictionary of Argot.) Warszawa: Osrodek Badan Przestepczosci Ministerstwa Sprawiedliwosci, Departament Szkolenia Wydawnictw MSW.

Miller, Walter B. 1958. Lower Class Culture as a Generating Milieu of Gang Delinquency. *Journal of Social Issues* 14: 5–19.

Moczydlowski, Pawel. 1992. *The Hidden Life of Polish Prisons.* Bloomington: Indiana University Press.

Mums. 1985a. Wiezienia PRL 1 (Polish Prisons 1). *Praworzadnosc* II (8/9):80–6.

Mums. 1985b. Wiezienia PRL 2 (Polish Prisons 2). *Praworzadnosc* II (10/11):76–88.

Mums. 1986a. Wiezienia PRL 3 (Polish Prisons 3). *Praworzadnosc* III (12/13):70–78.

Mums. 1986b. Wiezienia PRL 4 (Polish Prisons 4). *Praworzadnosc* III (14):96–108.

Niesiolowski, Stefan. 1989. *Wysoki brzeg.* (High Bank of a River.) Poznan: W Drodze.

Ordeshook, Peter C. 1986. *Game Theory and Political Theory.* Cambridge: Cambridge University Press.

Schrag, Clarence. 1961. A Preliminary Criminal Topology. *Pacific Sociological Review* 4:11–16.

Schrag, Clarence, 1961. A Preliminsry Criminal Topology. *Pacific Sociological Review* 4:11–16.

Slaski, Ludwik. 1992. *Lata wykreslone z zycia. Proces polityczny i wiezienia PRL.* (Years Erased from Life. Political Trials and Polish Prisons.) Krakow: Oficyna Literacka.

Solzhenitsyn, Alexander. 1979. *The Oak and the Calf.* New York: Harper and Row.

Stepniak, Klemens. 1993. *Slownik tajemnych gwar przestepczych.* (The Dictionary of Secret Criminal Argots.) London: Puls Publications lLd.

Stwora, Jacek. 1993. *Co jest za tym murem? (What is behind this wall?).* 1st ed. 1967. Krakow: Wydawnictwo Literackie.

Sykes, G. M. 1999. *The Society of Captives.* Princeton, N.J.: Princeton University Press. 1st ed. 1958.

Sykes, Gresham M., and Sheldon L. Messinger. 1960. The Inmate Social System. In *Theoretical Studies in Social Organization of the Prison,* edited by R. A. Cloward, D. R. Cressey, G. H. Grosser, R. McCleery, L. E. Ohlin, G. M. Sykes, and S. L. Messinger. New York: Social Science Research Council.

Thomas, Charles W., and David M. Petersen. 1977. *Prison Organization and Inmate Subcultures.* Indianapolis, IN: Bobbs-Merrill.

Trebicki, Jerzy [Jerzy Nasierowski] 1988. *Zbrodnia i. . .* (Crime and . . .) Krakow: Wydawnictwo Literackie.

Varese, Federico. 2001. *The Russian Mafia. Private Protection in a New Market Economy.* Oxford: Oxford University Press.

Wantchekon, Leonard, and Andrew Healy. 1999. The Game of Torture. *Journal of Conflict Resolution* 43 (2):230–43.

Wieclawski, Janusz. 2002. *Wiezienie zwane Popowem (Prison called Popowo)* Szuszkiewicz, Maciej (ed.). Available online at www.publikator.gower.pl.

Wojciechowski, Roman. 1981. Rok 1952. (1952) *Krytyka* 12:124–40.

Index

Unless otherwise indicated, words in italics denote prison terminology.